"Grief and loss are dreaded experiences that many wish to either avoid or to rapidly solve. In *Grieving Mindfully*, Kumar offers the alternative of welcoming the experience as an opportunity to develop our humanity. This book offers a path to healthy grieving for people encountering losses of many kinds."

—*Richard Tedeschi, Ph.D., professor of psychology at the University of North Carolina at Charlotte*

"Kumar's approach to dealing with grief and loss is creative and radically transformative. Drawing on his experience as a practicing psychologist and his training in the Buddhist enlightenment tradition, he suggests that instead of hiding from our grief, trying to forget or get over it, we take a more demanding and rewarding path—walking straight through grief with mindful awareness, fearless observance, and profound compassion. His book has the potential to bring strength and healing to the millions who grieve and to revolutionize the approach of psychologists and counselors working with those in profound grief."

—*Glenn H Mullin, Buddhist meditation teacher and author of* Living in the Face of Death: The Tibetan Tradition

grieving mindfully

A Compassionate and Spiritual Guide to Coping with Loss

SAMEET M. KUMAR, PH.D.

New Harbinger Publications, Inc.

Publisher's Note

This publication is designed to provide accurate and authoritative information in regard to the subject matter covered. It is sold with the understanding that the publisher is not engaged in rendering psychological, financial, legal, or other professional services. If expert assistance or counseling is needed, the services of a competent professional should be sought.

Excerpt on page 24 and 34 © Sarah Harding and Khenchen Thrangu Rinpoche, 1996, 2002. Excerpted from *Creation and Completion: Essential Points of Tantric Meditation* with permission of Wisdom Publications, 199 Elm St., Somerville, MA 02144, U.S.A., www.wisdompubs.org.

Excerpt on page 60 from *The Way of the Bodhisattva* by Shantideva, translated by the Padmakara Translation Group. © 1997 by the Padmakara Translation Group. Reprinted by arrangement with Shambhala Publications, Inc., Boston, www.shambhala.com.

Excerpt on page 19 © Shaykh Tosun Bayrak al-Jerrahi al-Halveti, from *The Name and the Named: The Divine Attributes of God*, with permission of Fons Vitae, Louisville, KY.

Copyright © 2005 by Sameet Kumar
New Harbinger Publications, Inc.
5674 Shattuck Avenue
Oakland, CA 94609
www.newharbinger.com

Cover design by Amy Shoup
Acquired by Tesilya Hanauer
Edited by Karen O'Donnell Stein
Text design by Tracy Marie Carlson

ISBN-10 1-57224-401-1
ISBN-13 978-1-57224-401-6

Library of Congress Cataloging in Publication Data on file
Distributed in Canada by Raincoast Books
All Rights Reserved

New Harbinger Publications' website address: www.newharbinger.com

Printed in the United States of America

20   19   18

30   29   28   27   26   25   24

I would like to dedicate this book to all of my patients and clients over the years, who have taught me so much about grief, loss, suffering, and the positive potential of being human. It is a privilege to know so many people capable of such deep caring and love for each other. You all renew my faith in humanity each day.

In this book, I have tried to communicate some of my own understanding of the Dharma, but in the end I am only a beginner, and the Dharma is vast. I beg the reader to overlook my errors. May this incomplete work, with all of its faults and shortcomings, be of assistance in easing the suffering of all beings everywhere.

Sarve mangalam.

Contents

Foreword

I am happy and honored to introduce Sameet Kumar and this book, *Grieving Mindfully*. In these pages, Sameet brings together a wealth of experience from the field of grief counseling and from his long-standing and dedicated personal practice of mindfulness meditation. He writes in a comprehensive yet inviting way, with warmth, humor, and great compassion. Most of all, Sameet offers an encouraging sense of hope when facing our own grief and loss. For the hope, I am especially grateful.

To be human is to be subject to the pain of loss and grief. The death of a loved one only heightens our remembrance of all the occasions and sources of loss throughout our lives. Whether it is the loss of a pet in childhood, good friends moving away, or the occurrence of illness in our own body, there is a real and deeply felt sense of grief connected to so many experiences.

Grief can be as unpredictable as it is intense. As a young psychiatry resident, I received a call from my mother informing me that her mother, my grandmother, had died from a sudden heart attack. Immediately on hearing the news, I noticed a numbing feeling beginning in my feet and moving upward through my entire body. After a few moments it was as if I were disconnected from my body, but could still hear my mother's voice on the other end of the phone. I felt disoriented and confused and could not explain why that reaction had occurred in me. I had no control over the reaction. Nothing like that had ever happened to me before, and has not since.

The experience of grief challenges our deepest sense of who we are. Without help and wisdom we can find ourselves severely and chronically disrupted by the reactions of fear, anger, and isolation arising from grief. Our sense of connection with life itself can seem to disappear.

Yet, though overwhelmed by the great upset of grief, we have a choice about how to respond. We can turn away from our own deep pain, seeking relief from distraction, numbing, and denial. Or we can turn toward the pain with compassionate attention and a willingness to allow what we are feeling to be just as it is.

Mindfulness enables us to turn toward the grief process and connect with the experience as it unfolds. As Sameet clearly advises, it is in connecting mindfully, even to painful experiences like grief, that the potential for transforming and enriching our lives exists.

Mindfulness is available to each of us. It is a basic human capacity. Mindfulness is an awareness that arises as we pay attention on purpose, nonjudgmentally, to unfolding experience in the present moment. The way of paying attention is crucial. Mindfulness is sensitive, warm, friendly, compassionate, and allowing. Mindful attention does not try to change what is happening. Instead, it reflects— accurately and precisely. Being mindful means being a witness to, and connecting consciously with, whatever elements of our life that are present now, in this moment.

Being mindful, we become the observers and experiencers of life, rather than its victims. We become witnesses to the ever-changing flow of the inner life instead of being carried away by the currents of our minds or the reactions of our bodies.

Grieving Mindfully introduces ancient and effective mindfulness practices and encourages us to use them to become more mindful of inner life as the grief process unfolds. We are also encouraged to become more mindful of the outer and everyday activities of living.

Getting to know life and the process of grief through mindfulness is crucial to the healing and transformation of the grief.

Through mindful attention, we discover the fact that grief is not who we are. Grief is not an identity. What feels so solid and real as a grief reaction (or any other reaction) in any moment is merely a combination of powerful reactive habits of thinking, feeling, and physical sensations. Learning to inhabit our awareness and deepen its scope by practicing mindfulness enables us to experience how much larger and more vibrant we actually are—beyond any experience or upset, even grief. And, by inhabiting each moment with compassionate awareness, we discover how capable we are of containing and healing the grief we carry.

The practice of mindfulness is not limited to Buddhists or to mystics or spiritual seekers of any single tradition. In my own work in mindfulness-based stress reduction, I have seen individuals from all faith traditions and walks of life benefit from the practice of mindfulness. The benefits arise in any aspect of a person's life when compassionate, nonjudging attention is applied. Paradoxically, the benefits depend not upon trying to change anything, but instead mainly upon one's willingness and commitment to reside in the present moment, while making room and becoming intimate with the texture of unfolding experience—whatever that is.

So, in conclusion, I would like to thank Sameet for this valuable and important book. He offers us a map, a vocabulary, and a methodology for encountering grief and—surprise—becoming wiser and more alive as a result.

I am glad you have found *Grieving Mindfully*. I hope you will keep it handy. Allow yourself to digest it slowly. Keep it as a medicine for dying and for living.

May the intelligence and practices of this book inform and comfort you. May mindfulness grow in your life. May your grief be transformed and your wisdom benefit the entire world.

> —Jeffrey Brantley, MD, Director, Mindfulness-Based Stress Reduction Program
> Duke Center for Integrative Medicine, Durham, N.C.

Acknowledgments

So many people, so many relationships, have made this work possible. First and foremost, I would like to thank all of my spiritual teachers, without whom life would truly be void of meaning and direction: Shri Das Gupta, Shri Shastriji (Guruji); Swami Nityananda and Swami Muktananda, His Holiness the Dalai Lama, Shri Brahmananda Saraswati, and Lama Norla Rinpoche; Sogyal Rinpoche, Jamgon Kongtrul, and Chogyam Trungpa Rinpoche, from whom I have learned so much from a distance; and the Tibetan Library of Miami.

I want to thank my family, a constant source of support and inspiration, and Christina—my wife, my best friend, and my valiant editor, who took time away from her own book to help me with mine. This work would not have been possible without her feedback, patience, support, and love. Javier Amrit, the new light of our world. My parents, my sisters, and their families, who have brought me so much love and joy. All of my in-laws, especially Elsa and Marlene for their hours of babysitting. All of my friends and companions over the years, many of whom have journeyed on, and many of whom are still with me.

The seed of grief in my life—my maternal grandparents, Ram Rahki and Atma Ram, and Uncle Raj, and the millions of others who died and suffered—Hindu, Muslim, Sikh, Christian—in the Partition of the Indian subcontinent, the unspoken Holocaust of 1947. The Loma Prieta earthquake and Hurricane Andrew.

I would not be where I am if Dr. Raul Birnbaum, Dr. Noel Q. King, and Dr. Mischael Caspi had not taught me how to meditate on the text, and Dr. G. William Domhoff had not supported, encouraged, and guided me to remember my dreams and "follow my bliss." To the University of California, Santa Cruz, for making it all come together so many years ago, and the University of Miami for helping me to connect the dots.

This work would not have come together had I not had the support and understanding of my amazing colleagues at the Mt. Sinai Comprehensive Cancer Center; they constantly seek out new frontiers of compassion and service. Thanks to Philip Mandel for his helpful feedback on earlier drafts.

Special thanks to the musicians who inspired me during this project—Miles Davis, Fela Anikulapo-Kuti and the Africa 70, Ud. Nusrat Fateh Ali Khan and Party, DJ Cheb i Sabbah, Midival Punditz, Prince Paul, Birds of Avalon, and the Grateful Dead.

I would like to extend my profound gratitude to the entire staff at New Harbinger, especially Catharine Sutker, for believing in this project and trusting me with this work, and my editor, Karen Stein, for her priceless feedback. I would also like to thank Dr. Peter Campos, Nishan Mahendran, Daniel Fox, and Ana and Lorenzo González for their integral roles in the process of creating and completing this work.

Introduction

Loss is a part of everyone's life. We suffer loss in many ways: separation, divorce, unemployment, relocation, immigration, natural disaster, illness, and death. None of us will leave this life without first losing relationships that matter. However, despite skyrocketing divorce rates, the rise of many life-threatening diseases, and the aging of our parents (and ourselves), we still have a hard time talking about how we feel about these losses. As American society approaches unparalleled material wealth and technological progress, we seem to be losing a sense of meaning and purpose in our lives.

Grief offers us all an opportunity to pause and look at the deeper questions of life, to find personal meaning and purpose.

WHO THIS BOOK IS FOR

If you are reading this book, chances are that you are already feeling the uncomfortable emotions that follow loss and are wishing to navigate your way through grief carefully. This book offers guidance on how to cope with the ups and downs of grief.

But this book is about much more than grief. It also offers you insight on how to live life with more richness and more meaning. You will learn techniques to help you pick up the pieces of your life and to keep living with the richness that comes from asking the deeper questions about life and suffering.

This book is for anyone who is suffering from the loss of a relationship and wants to experience grief as a positive, life-changing journey, even though it may still be quite difficult emotionally.

My own experiences with grief cover a broad spectrum. One such experience was the sudden loss of a relationship that was very dear to me. To help me cope with my loss, I went back to India to attend some teachings being given by His Holiness the Dalai Lama. These teachings had a profound effect on me, both personally and professionally. They helped me solidify my daily meditation practice, make several life-changing decisions, find my career path as a clinical psychologist, and make many other beneficial changes in my life.

Most of my professional experience with loss and grief comes from my work at the Mt. Sinai Comprehensive Cancer Center in Miami Beach, Florida. As you might expect, much of my work entails navigating concerns about death and dying, even with the many people who survive cancer.

Through my personal and professional experiences, I have learned that no matter what the cause, grief is grief. For some people, the death of a loved one may not be as devastating as the end of a marriage. Everyone grieves, and grief tends to be more similar than different. I use the words *death* and *loss* almost interchangeably throughout the book because each time we suffer a loss, a part of our identity dies—and is transformed. In this way, death, a final loss, is a metaphor for all of the other types of loss we experience in life. What is most important is not the type or cause of grief, but how you feel, the changes you make along the way, and how you choose to live afterward.

In navigating through my own grief personally and professionally, I have learned that there are often life-changing treasures to be discovered in places you would least expect them. I wrote this book, with an understanding of the pain you might be feeling, in order to help you find your own treasures.

BUDDHISM AND PSYCHOLOGY

Even though many of the ideas and practices I present herein are of Buddhist origin, you certainly don't have to be a Buddhist to benefit from them. In fact, psychologists are finding that many of the ideas traditionally considered to be Buddhist, such as mindfulness and meditation, can be effectively integrated into psychotherapy.

As both a Buddhist and a psychotherapist, I find that there are often more similarities than differences between these two conceptual systems. Fundamentally, Buddhism and psychotherapy have a shared focus: to alleviate suffering. This is also the focus of many of the world's spiritual traditions. Both Buddhism and psychotherapy aim to alleviate suffering by changing how we look at the world, and by challenging the fundamental assumptions that we use to construct our realities.

Buddhism and psychotherapy both place emphasis on being an active participant in your life. You cannot merely read about mindfulness; you have to practice the technique. Similarly, visiting and listening to a therapist are not much help unless you are willing to disclose your feelings and participate in the therapeutic process. For this reason, I repeatedly emphasize the importance of maintaining a regular mindfulness practice, whether it be formal meditation, or transforming an everyday task into a meditation ritual.

A Note about Buddhist Texts

Throughout the book, I draw extensively from the teachings of the Buddha, which were compiled by his disciples shortly after his death. These teachings were called *suttas* in the colloquial Pali language of the day, or *sutras* in the more formal Sanskrit language. Some of the names of the suttas can be quite difficult for English-speaking readers, but, thankfully, you will not be quizzed on them.

THE PURPOSE OF THIS BOOK

This book has one main purpose: to help you grieve by using mindfulness as your guide and emotional and spiritual resilience as your goals. Mindfulness helps you to be aware of all the moments of your life and your relationships, your hopes and your dreams, all of which have been shaken up by loss. Grieving mindfully is the process of putting the pieces back together consciously, while appreciating who or what you have lost, who you are, and who you want to be.

The purpose of this book is to encourage you to look at loss, grief, and spirituality not as the end of a journey but as potent vehicles for personal transformation and inner growth. Although loss often makes you feel as if a door has closed on a relationship, in time you will see that actually a new door has been opened—one that leads to the rest of your life.

HOW TO USE THIS BOOK

This book is designed to be interactive. I highly recommend that you keep a journal or notebook with you as you read this book and perform these exercises. Almost all of the people that I work with benefit from journaling during the first months, and even years, after suffering loss. Journaling and writing through this process is important not only in the here and now but also in the future. I guarantee that after your distress has worn off, you will treasure the insights and observations that you keep in this journal.

Although the book is meant to help you move deeper into the meaning of your life, it is also designed to alleviate your suffering as you make that journey. However, keep in mind that grief is not always predictable, linear, or logical; each time a milestone approaches and passes, you may find old emotions stirred up again.

Similarly, the practice of mindfulness is also not linear. You may at first develop a certain level of mindfulness, only to then feel as though you can no longer reach this state. On the other hand, you may find that the longer you practice, the better you understand certain concepts such as radical acceptance. For this reason, in life and in this book, aspects of mindfulness are revealed gradually, to better reflect your experience with the practice. Several themes and topics are then revisited throughout the book to help you build upon your deepening understanding of the process of mindfulness.

You may also find yourself wanting to review certain sections or chapters even if you have already read them. For instance, you may have to refer to chapter 2 repeatedly to brush up on mindfulness skills. Reading chapter 3 may be very helpful to you around holidays or anniversaries. The information in chapters 6 and 7 may help you during times when the pain of grief seems particularly intense, or if you are feeling helpless to identify your thoughts. And you may want to refer to chapters 8 and 9 again and again to inform your spiritual path.

The lessons of grief do not go away. It is my hope that this book will help to point you in the right direction for living a more meaningful, compassionate life.

I

What Is Grief?

Grief is a personal journey, never the same for any two people, and as unique as your life and your relationships.

Grief may be the experience of continuing to love someone after they die, of longing for a loved one's presence, and yet knowing that it is no longer available. Even though you mourn the person's passing, you may still feel toward that person as you do toward your living loved ones: you may still cherish, resent, or long for your their company, and feel frustrated by the loss you have experienced.

However, grief is not limited to loss through death. Every time you lose a relationship or are faced with uncertainty, you grieve the loss of a predictable and safe world. You experience grief when you move to a new town, lose a job, or go through a divorce. You experience grief when you are diagnosed with a life-changing illness, or when you are separated from a loved one by circumstance. You experience grief when you experience any change in your relationship to the world.

Grief can seem overwhelming at times. You may feel helpless when you are flooded by emotions that are triggered by a memory, by a song being played in a store, or by watching other people enjoying each other. It may seem too intense to bear. You may feel as though you have only two choices, either to be swept up by the intensity of your grief or to shield yourself from the pain. Paradoxically, it is often when you try to resist intense emotions that they linger, and even hurt more deeply when they inevitably surface.

As I discussed in the introduction, the intense pain of grief is temporary. You will feel better in time. However, it is *how* you decide to feel better, and *what* you do with your pain, that are the focus of this book. In my work with the bereaved, I have helped many people use their grief to their benefit, to open up their lives to new horizons while working with loss. I would like to help you to do the same: give meaning to your loss by transforming your grief into a reaffirmation of life.

WHAT IS GRIEVING MINDFULLY?

Grieving mindfully can be understood as being consciously aware of the intense pain of love after loss. This may sound a bit strange at first, since the pain can seem to be swallowing you up, and you may feel that you are all too aware of it, often to the point of not being aware of anything else. Such emotions can make it difficult to find meaning in your existence and can rob you of a sense of purpose and direction. You are probably already feeling some of the intense emotional pain of grief and are wondering why you would possibly want to be aware of its intensity.

Awareness is not the same as indulging in the intensity of grief, nor is allowing yourself to come into full contact with your thoughts and feelings after loss the same as wallowing in pain, or keeping yourself in pain. Awareness is allowing yourself to accept the pain of grief, thereby finding relief in not running away from your loss. Grieving mindfully is the process of using your emotional vulnerability not to suffer greater distress, or to intensify your pain, but to redirect this pain toward your growth as a human being. Engaging in this process begins when you come in full contact with yourself and learn to ride the waves of grief. Your thoughts, your feelings, your identity after loss all become vehicles for your own evolution. Grieving mindfully can be understood as making the decision to allow yourself to mourn, and to fully experience the lessons of grief with the goal of living life better.

The terrible emotional pain of grief tends to have a life and process of its own. Allowing the process to unfold with mindful awareness—a sense of purpose and direction to the pain—may not remove all distress, but it can soften the sharp edge of pain. To allow the process means to allow yourself to feel and experience each day on its own terms; we cannot assume that we know what tomorrow will bring.

As you are experiencing this process, you will feel that very natural pull to escape or numb yourself from the pain. However, by being aware of grief rather than ignoring or denying it, and by working to understand what drives this pain, you can release yourself into the person you are and the person you want to be. In other words, with mindful awareness of your grief, you can move closer to the people in your life who matter the most, and change habits or ideas that have been keeping you from living fully. Full awareness, especially in grief, of your patterns of thought, feelings, and behavior can take you from living with misery, fear, and discontent to living with openness and passion.

Simply put, grieving mindfully enables us to use the tremendous influx of emotional energy that comes from experiencing loss to nurture life. Grieving mindfully means approaching your grief as an opportunity to grow by actively giving meaning to your pain.

Channeling the momentum of grief into a journey of awakening is difficult if you are trying to rush the process or if you become completely numb to your feelings. Well-meaning friends may encourage us to "move on," or "get on with life." Yet when we are told to "get over it," a very subtle but profound message is being given to us: that we are doing something wrong by grieving. If you can understand grief as an extension of love, then you will see that there is nothing wrong with grieving. To deny the importance of grieving would be saying that there is something pathological about loving.

BUDDHISM AND GRIEF

Traditional accounts of the life story of the Buddha include an episode that illustrates the relationship between love and grief, as well as the universality of grief—the story of a young mother named Krisha Gotami, who lived at the time of the Buddha.

Krisha Gotami's only child, a baby, became sick and died. Grief stricken, she held the tiny, lifeless body close to her heart and wandered weeping through the streets, asking everyone she met if they could help her. Someone told her that the only person who could help her was the Buddha, who was giving teachings outside the city.

Krisha Gotami went to the forest grove where the Buddha was preaching. Reverently, she presented the lifeless body to him and, with tears in her eyes, asked if he could bring her baby back to life.

After contemplating her request for some moments, the Buddha consented, but with a condition: she would need to bring him a single mustard seed from a household that had never been visited by death before he would grant her request.

Ecstatic, Krisha Gotami went to the city. She knocked on the door of every single house, rich or poor. People answered, "My grandfather died last year," "My son died just last month," "My husband died ten years ago," and "My cousin was killed when he was a child."

Krisha Gotami went through the entire city looking for that mustard seed, but she could not find a single household that had not been visited by death. Finally, she understood what the Buddha was trying to tell her. She brought her baby to the cremation grounds and gazed upon the tiny body for the last time. After the cremation, she joined the disciples of the Buddha. It is said that she became enlightened before her own death many years later.

When we experience death or loss on a personal level, we forget the hard truth of Krisha Gotami's story: that death and loss are inevitable, and grief is natural. They are so unavoidable and common in all of our lives that not a single household has escaped their touch. However, although we may never understand why death occurs, we can learn to accept loss and grief as natural processes. Like Krisha Gotami, we may first have to become aware of how much suffering this world holds for everyone else before we can accept our own. But, also like Krisha Gotami, once we accept the universality of loss and grief, we can set ourselves free from the bondage of pain and place ourselves on the path of our spiritual evolution.

The inevitability of death and loss became the cornerstone of the Buddha's teaching. The first of his Four Noble Truths states simply that life is wrought with suffering. This is not just the profound suffering of death; it is also petty suffering—of not getting what we want, of always desiring more, of living without pleasure, or living with emotional, physical, or spiritual pain. For the Buddha, the idea of a perfect and comfortable life was a grand illusion; suffering is what we experience when this illusion vanishes. Because we all buy into this illusion at some point in our lives, suffering is a natural law. We simply don't always get what we want, and so we suffer.

Grief Happens

From this perspective, then, there is nothing "wrong" with you if you are grieving. Grief is a part of life. This is a very different perspective from that of our pleasure-driven, youth-oriented society. Most of us, in societies around the world, have a tendency to associate suffering and distress with something being wrong. We all inherently want to experience pleasure and avoid pain. Yet suffering is a part of all of our lives, and, although not desirable, it will happen no matter what we do. If we view grief as a problem, we will think of one of the most natural parts of life, *and love,* as a pathology or "disorder." But grief has always been part of the order of things, and it always will be. As part of suffering, grief too is a natural law.

Why We Grieve

My years of work with people suffering loss through illness and death have shown me again and again that love and grief are inextricably intertwined—to love is always to open oneself to the grief of loss. However, this loss is not to be confused with the loss *of* love. Grief is the experience of loss *in* love.

Simply put, it is only without love that there is no grief. Love is the fuel that drives grief. Rather than point to a deficit or weakness, grief only serves to highlight the depth of our capacity to love and be loved. Just as love depends on the courage to share yourself with another person, grieving mindfully depends on the courage to accept your own feelings.

The relationship between grief and love is easy to forget when you are suffering. By practicing mindfulness, you will find the natural place of grief in your life. I believe that this place is in your heart, side by side with the role of love in your life.

Suffering and frustrated desire are a part of life, but *how* we respond to them—how we grieve—can vary greatly. Moreover, how we respond can enable us to also experience much satisfaction and enjoyment in life.

TYPES OF GRIEF

Although grief is a universal experience, there are many different types of grief. Each of these kinds of grief colors the grieving process for you, as do your personal experiences with loss during your life. The next few sections explore some common types of grief that many of us will experience in our lives.

Cumulative Grieving

Loss can happen in many ways. Someone we love might change and no longer want to see us. Or a loved one may move away, thus changing the nature of our relationship. We may move away, or change, and be unable to sustain the relationship. Or a loved one may die.

Grief often has a cumulative quality to it. Whenever we lose a loved one, be it through a broken relationship or death, we tend to reexperience our previous losses. This is especially the case for people who work with suffering on a daily basis. If you are a doctor or nurse, psychologist or social worker, or chaplain or counselor, or if you work in law enforcement, the military, or any other profession that brings you into contact with death and suffering on a daily basis, a personal loss can seem particularly overwhelming. When we experience a personal loss, the scars from our previous losses can open up again. However, each of our losses can also teach us how to cope better with suffering.

To better understand the cumulative grief you may be feeling, take some time now to list on a piece of paper some of the more painful losses you have suffered in your life. Those past losses may pale in comparison to what you are feeling now, but you may be reexperiencing some of the feelings associated with those losses. Jot down the details and circumstances of each loss. Note how old you were, and whether the event was the result of a broken heart, a move to a different town, the loss of a job or home, divorce, or death. How did each of these losses feel? Note how you coped with the losses. Did you find another relationship, try to numb yourself with drugs or alcohol, seek psychotherapy, or change your lifestyle? Were you happy with how you coped? And are you reexperiencing any feelings from your previous losses at the present time?

In order to get an appreciation of how much loss is a part of life, and see how often you've dealt with it in the past, take particular note of how many losses you have experienced over the years. Also pay attention to how you were—or weren't—able to overcome the pain of these losses. It is especially important to focus on the healthy ways in which you were able to cope with the losses. If you were not able to cope in ways you found satisfactory, note this also. Finally, take a look at your list and notice whether any familiar patterns emerge.

Cumulative grief is a process that I have observed in many people, including myself. It can feel overwhelming and yet familiar, and it can magnify the intensity of your feelings so that they become disproportionate to your current situation. Mindfulness can help you identify the sources of your thoughts and feelings, allowing you to generate a clearer understanding and experience of your own personal grief process.

Anticipatory Grief

We have all experienced a form of anticipatory grief at some point in our lives. When we are children, the end of summer vacation brings with it fears about the future—the inevitable return to school. When one of our relationships is disintegrating, we fearfully anticipate the loss of other relationships. When our vacations or holidays are ending, we dread the return to our work and our daily routines. When a loved one is suffering with illness or disability for some time, we begin to grieve before the death in anticipation of the loss to come. The profound uncertainty regarding the future—cure versus death, hope versus hopelessness—makes it impossible for most people in this situation to focus clearly on the here and now.

Anticipatory grief often begins the day of the initial diagnosis or symptoms of a life-threatening illness. On one level, you may have grieved your loved one's decline in health, or certain things that he or she was no longer able to do around the house. You may have grieved the loss of normal routines that did not involve the hospital or doctor's visits, such as grocery shopping or watching TV together. You may have grieved no longer being able to go out for a spontaneous meal without having to plan around medication schedules or deal with physical limitations.

On another level, a diagnosis of a life-threatening illness brings an intense intimacy with death and impermanence that does not limit itself to the person suffering from the disease. When your loved one was diagnosed, you may have felt a host of conflicting emotions: helplessness or frustration, sadness, anger, guilt, anxiety, and exhaustion. You may have experienced constant dread and anticipation, even while trying to be patient, encouraging, and understanding. You may have found it impossible to attend to yourself. Everyone experiences anticipatory grief differently. Though it is always painful, it is different for everyone.

Research shows that the nearly constant stress of being a caregiver can have a dramatic impact on your health and well-being (Shulz and Martire 2004). In some cases, caregiving can even be considered a trauma, along the lines of a car crash or terrorist attack. As a result, the actual moment of your loved one's passing may have felt like more of a relief than a loss.

You may have even wished that your ailing loved one would die, and you probably feel a considerable amount of guilt over this. I have found, for most of the people I have worked with, this is actually a strong wish that their loved one's suffering would stop. It is an exhausting sense of helplessness that makes us wish for their death.

More important, anticipatory grief plays a central role in the process of grief. Therese A. Rando (1997) suggests that anticipatory grief helps us to accomplish two crucial psychological tasks: 1) to understand that your loved one might not live, and 2) to prepare your mind for a future without your loved one in it. In many ways, while you experienced the waiting of anticipatory grief, you were preparing yourself for your loved one's death on mental, emotional, spiritual, and physical levels. Like grief in general, anticipatory grief is a natural process.

In cases of a loved one's prolonged illness, it can be nearly impossible to focus clearly on the here and now because you are always waiting for the future to happen. Even after the death, you may still find yourself waiting to get through your grief, a holiday, or a social obligation. Mindfulness can help you get reacquainted with the vast potential of each moment of your life—it is the antidote to the endless waiting for tomorrow.

Post-Traumatic Stress Disorder

Many people who suffer traumatic loss can find the experience of day-to-day life difficult precisely because they are a survivor. Post-traumatic stress disorder (PTSD) was acknowledged by psychologists as a genuine ailment after some veterans of the Vietnam War found it difficult to return to a "normal" life. However, PTSD is not limited to Vietnam War veterans, or to the experience of combat. People who suffer from PTSD may have survived a car accident, a natural catastrophe like a hurricane or earthquake, a fire, a physical or sexual assault, or any other instance in which your or someone else's life was threatened or in danger. And many mental-health practitioners now consider nursing a loved one through illness or seeing him or her dying to be a trauma that can lead to PTSD.

The term PTSD is a diagnostic category used by mental-health professionals. People who are diagnosed with PTSD itself have experienced or witnessed an event when their or someone else's life was in danger and felt fear, helplessness, or horror. In addition, they reexperience the event by 1) having recurrent or intrusive thoughts about it; 2) having recurrent distressing dreams; 3) momentarily acting or feeling as if the event were reoccurring (known as a "flashback"); or 4) experiencing psychological or physiological distress upon internal or external reminders of the event.

PTSD sufferers avoid things that remind them of the trauma by doing or experiencing three or more of the following that they didn't do before the trauma: 1) avoiding thoughts, feelings, or conversations about the event; 2) avoiding people, places, and activities that remind them about the event; 3) being unable to remember parts of the event; 4) not feeling like doing their normal activities; 5) feeling detached from others; 6) not being able to feel a full range of emotions; and 7) feeling as if their future is shortened (e.g., not making any long-term plans).

In addition to the above, they also acquire two or more of the following new symptoms: 1) difficulty falling or staying asleep, 2) irritability or outbursts of anger, 3) difficulty concentrating, 4) hypervigilance, and 5) an exaggerated startle response.

People who are diagnosed with PTSD have experienced the specific combinations of the symptoms listed above for at least a month, to such a degree that they significantly impair their ability to function in daily life. It is important to remember that not everyone who witnesses suffering or trauma should be diagnosed with PTSD, but there is nothing wrong with you if you are.

Even if you are not diagnosed with PTSD, you may experience some of these symptoms after you witness suffering, especially if it is long or intense. It is also easy to overidentify with a loved one's diagnosis. However, if you feel that you have, or might have, PTSD, it is important that you find a skilled mental-health practitioner who can help you through these symptoms, since the treatment of PTSD is outside the scope of this book.

Unhealthy Ways of Coping

You may feel compelled to try unhealthy ways of coping now more than ever. If you have a past or present alcohol or drug abuse problem, grief may bring back forgotten cravings. Similarly, if you have or have had unhealthy or abusive relationships, the pain of grief may make you long for the familiarity of these unhealthy relationships. These are all ways to cope with the grief of loss that ultimately will probably not be beneficial.

STAGES OF GRIEF?

Historically, psychologists have tended to think about grief within a relatively rigid framework. At one time there was even an expectation that the initial pain of grief should wear off in less than two months. Yet in my years of working with the bereaved, I have *never* found two months to be a realistic expectation. In fact, we are now learning that two *years* may be a more realistic amount of time in which to begin to regain resilience. Healthy grief does not usually progress in predictable stages. As many therapists, including me, have discovered, grief can actually be very unpredictable. Because most human beings cherish their relationships and have an intense capacity for love, when this love is transformed into grief it defies logical timetables or expectations. The fact that a certain amount of time has gone by does not mean you should be feeling a certain way. Similarly, the fact that you have experienced a certain emotion for a long period of time does not mean you won't feel it again.

Grief is nonlinear; it can't be illustrated by a straight line on a chart, or by universally identifiable stages. Although there may be phases of intensity or certain themes in your grief journey, it is likely that these phases will be unique to your life. Because no one follows the same path in grieving, this book does not talk about "stages" of grief. Rather, we will talk about the ups and downs, the ebb and flow, of grief.

I conceptualize grief as a free-form, curving line that often takes the shape of a spiral staircase. This is the simplest way to illustrate how unpredictable and sometimes repetitive grief can be. What the spiral is made up of depends on your own personal experiences. The ups and downs in the spiral can be triggered by certain people or situations and are not limited to a particular timeline. Your emotions may repeat, or they may disappear quickly. When the process occurs in a healthy way, it tends to move forward and upward toward growth and vitality. By going through grief, many of us find a new relationship to life and those around us.

My professional experiences with nonlinear, upward-moving healthy grief are not unique. In fact, recent research (Bonanno 2004) shows that most of us have an innate tendency toward healthy grief and recovery from loss. This means that we tend to emerge from grief stronger than we were when we went into it. This does not mean that grief does not hurt, or that you do not suffer or stumble along the way. Rather, it suggests that at the end of your long and unique journey through tremendous emotional pain, you have the capacity to grow, love, and thrive. Like suffering and grief, resilience—which means having the elasticity and buoyancy to recover from the experience of enduring suffering and pain—may also be a part of the natural order.

If your grief is new, you may feel discouraged by reading that resilience is natural, and ask yourself, "If resilience is so easy and natural, why am I having such a hard time?" Please keep in mind that an end result of resilience does not mean the journey will be quick or easy. Resilience is the perspective you will have after you feel better. If you are able to use your grief for self-improvement, you will describe yourself as "resilient." Give yourself time to become resilient; it cannot be rushed. Everyone has the potential to be resilient, even if you don't feel that this term describes you now.

SPIRITUALITY AND GRIEF

Although the study of resilience is new to modern science, this concept has long been a part of the world's great spiritual traditions, especially in the context of being aware of our mortality. The goal of resilience in the face of death and impermanence has frequently been used to motivate people to cultivate compassion, spirituality, and ethical behavior. In reminding us of our fleeting existence, the great spiritual traditions are trying to harness the power of grief to bring us closer to each other and to improve our lives. They are using grief to help us bounce back into a richer way of living. In the mystical tradition of

Islam known as Sufism, Shaykh Tosun Bayrak (2000), building on the work of the renowned Al-Ghazali, said, "Only when the bird of your soul flies from the cage of the flesh will this dream evaporate, and you will find yourself alone with your deeds . . . Then you will know that what you presumed to be good was Hell, and what you thought was suffering was Paradise."

The Hebrew Bible succinctly characterizes the relationship between death and spirituality: "Even though I walk through the valley of the shadow of death, I fear no evil; for you are with me; your rod and your staff—they comfort me" (Ps. 23:4).

In Tibetan Buddhism, contemplating the certainty of death and the uncertainty about the actual time of death are considered the essential foundations of preliminary practice. The great Tibetan saint Togmey Zangpo, in his *Thirty-seven Practices of the Bodhisattva* (Gyeltsen 1989), wrote about the fact that all of our relationships eventually end, either through separation or death. Of all our accumulated wealth and possessions, no matter how expensive or cheap they are, we can take none with us, not even our body, at the end of our life.

Even though all of the above writings come from very different spiritual traditions, they all utilize awareness of death—in other words, grief—to accelerate our spiritual development. Seen from a psychospiritual point of view, healthy grief involves utilizing the pain that results from the loss of a loved one in order to become a better person, and trusting yourself to travel through intense pain in order to reemerge as a better person.

2

What Is Mindfulness?

Mindfulness is the act of being aware of the present moment—for instance, right now, being aware of the movement of your eyes across this page, the position of your body as you read this book, and your breath as it moves in and out of your body.

MINDFULNESS AND GRIEF

Mindfulness is the foundation of Buddhism, as well as many other spiritual and religious traditions of Asia. The following story about the origins of Buddhism may help you to understand the close relationship between mindfulness and grief.

The Buddha started his life as a rich prince born to a noble family. He was kept sheltered in opulence and leisure in his father's palace. At the age of twenty-nine, he ventured outside the confines of his home and encountered an elderly person disfigured by aging and arthritis, a sick person covered with boils and sores, and a corpse—all for the first time in his life. As his assumptions about the world being healthy, happy, safe, and fair were shattered, he encountered a wandering ascetic who seemed truly joyful and centered despite the suffering around him. To endeavor to understand the mystery of death and suffering in human life, the Buddha renounced his sheltered life, leaving behind his parents, his wife, and his newborn son. In one night, he lost everything that he had known his life to be. He lost his identity. He chose instead to wander through India, hoping to become one of the ascetics who seemed to have grasped the meaning of life and death.

After years of practicing severe austerities, he understood that the answers he sought could not be found in either decadence or self-mortification; after having lived through both extremes, he still had not found the answers he was looking for. The answer had been in front of him all along: the present moment. He sat down underneath a tree in the forest to meditate, and he vowed not to move until he was either enlightened or dead.

After seven days of mindfulness meditation, overcoming every distraction and obstacle in his way, he became completely enlightened. He saw clearly into the nature of life, even to the point of knowing the lives of all beings in the past, present, and future, throughout the universe. He experienced the full potential of a single moment. He became awake. From then on, he was known as "Buddha," Sanskrit for the "Awakened One."

Mindfulness is a way of experiencing life that has a unique relationship to grief: it was in encountering the sufferings of old age, sickness, and death—the losses of youth, health, and life itself—that the Buddha began his journey of awakening through the practice of mindfulness.

WHY GRIEVE MINDFULLY?

You may wonder what role mindfulness can play in helping you in the grieving process. My experience in working with hundreds of people who have lost loved ones, and my experiences in working through the losses in my own life, have shown me that grief ultimately teaches everyone the same lesson: to value the relationships, experiences, and time that you have in this present moment. This lesson is also the essence of mindfulness. By practicing mindfulness, you can experience grief as a purposeful, meaningful journey. Mindfulness can help give the intensity and distress of grief a positive role in transforming the rest of your life.

Understanding Mindfulness

Mindfulness is often described as a meditation practice, but in actuality it is a way of life. There are many different ways to meditate, and many different opportunities to practice mindfulness. You can practice mindfulness while walking, sweeping, peeling fruit, or preparing a meal. Any activity, when done mindfully, becomes a meditation session and can help you gain experiences that can serve as the building blocks of a mindful way of living.

Mindfulness meditation is often referred to as a "practice" for a very important reason. Mindfulness, even for the experienced, is rarely simple or perfect; rather, it is something that we practice again and again. Those who meditate or practice mindfulness regularly consider themselves to be "in training." Buddhist monks often refer to themselves as beginners even if they have been meditating for decades. Because mindfulness is constantly evolving, it always has the capacity to be a new experience, no matter how long we have been acquainted with it.

I recommend that you read this chapter in its entirety before either sitting down to practice or deciding it's not for you. It is important to have the right understanding of mindfulness before accepting or rejecting it.

Misconceptions of Mindfulness

In my years of teaching mindfulness meditation, especially to those who are feeling deep emotional pain, I have come across some common misconceptions of what mindfulness is all about, which may get in the way of understanding mindfulness.

The most common misconception is that you have to "empty your mind." This is impossible, especially when you are distressed. Your mind will be constantly thinking about your loved one, recently strained relationships, financial concerns, or daily tasks that seem overwhelming. You may have thoughts about the meaning of life, the existence of God, or folding the laundry. Mindfulness does not require us to stop all of these thoughts, but to be aware of them.

I have found the following verse by the nineteenth century Tibetan Buddhist master Jamgon Kongtrul Rinpoche very helpful in clarifying this misconception:

> You try to block thoughts and yet they are not blocked—
> first one unblocked thought arises, then a second—let
> them arise. When they arise, send them wherever they go
> and stand guard. Since there is no place for them to go,
> they have returned, like a crow who has taken off from a
> ship. Rest like the movements of swells at sea.
> (Harding and Thrangu 2002)

What Kongtrul Rinpoche is asking us to do is to be open to our experience, and to expect that we will, as usual, become distracted. In fact, mindfulness assumes that you will be distracted. I always congratulate my clients who, after being taught mindfulness meditation, come back and tell me that they did it a few times but were really distracted each time. The fact that they were distracted actually shows that they were paying attention. We are always distracted, but practicing mindfulness makes us aware of our distractions. Bringing your mind back to the present moment is mindfulness, and this would not be possible were it not for distraction.

The next most common misconception is that mindfulness or meditation will somehow make everything better immediately. This is unfortunately not the case. The goal of mindfulness is not to help you cover up the pain, but to help you be okay with being yourself. In the context of mindfulness, pain and pleasure are treated equally, and only with awareness. (This should not be confused with trying to hold on to the pain. It is not my intention to encourage you to either dwell in your pain or deny it. My intention is to help you weather the ups and downs of this incredibly intense emotional and spiritual journey.)

Just as you may have some good days during your grief, you may have some good sessions of mindfulness. You will also have some tough days during your grief, and you will sometimes have a tough time meditating. Just as grief is difficult to predict, so are moments of mindful awareness.

During mindfulness meditation, it is important to remain open to whatever is happening. If you have an easy session or an easy day, enjoy it. If you have a tough session or difficult day, allow it to happen. There is no way to predict how each session will go, just as you can't predict how you will feel next week. The practice of mindfulness helps you to stay present in one moment at a time when you are faced with many uncertainties about the future. You will undoubtedly experience many different types of thoughts and feelings in your mindfulness practice. Although it is important to be open to your experiences while practicing mindfulness, if you find yourself having frequent and recurring thoughts about hurting yourself or someone else, you should seek professional help as soon as possible.

Often, I find that people hold the assumption that, once they read or learn about mindfulness, the practice will unfold effortlessly. It is easy to forget that mindfulness is often hard work, requiring both effort and commitment. Mindfulness may not be an easy routine to establish. As you begin to practice mindfulness meditation, you may even feel awkward at first. You may also find yourself procrastinating when it's time to meditate. The task of sitting down with yourself to simply witness passing moments is difficult to accept in our society. We are more comfortable living on autopilot, missing the passing scenery as we run from one place to the next, mentally and physically. Mindfulness is simply the task of paying attention along the way.

HOW DO I PRACTICE MINDFULNESS?

Following the breath is the foundation of mindfulness practice, whether you are doing a formal meditation, or peeling an orange. When you are anxious, tense, or distressed, you tend to take relatively shallow breaths that are centered in the chest. You may feel that you are getting enough air, since you are using your lungs, but in reality, this is an inefficient way to breathe. When you cry, or have a panic attack, you breathe in short gasps centered in the chest. In contrast, when you are relaxed, at peace, or sleeping, you tend to take deep breaths centered in your belly. As you do this, you are actually supplying your blood with more oxygen because you are using your diaphragm to fill your lungs more completely with air. This is called "diaphragmatic breathing," or "belly breathing". Athletes, singers, and dancers make use of this technique, because it makes the body focused and efficient.

To practice mindfulness, you will need to develop diaphragmatic breathing skills. To do this, put one hand on your chest and one hand on your belly. As you breathe, try to make the hand on your belly move out as you inhale, and in as you exhale. Allow your belly to guide the air in and out of your body. The hand on your chest should move only slightly; let your belly do the work.

In order to follow diaphragmatic breaths, you need to give proper attention to how and where the body is placed during meditation. Here are some general guidelines:

- Avoid taking caffeine, alcohol, and drugs before meditating.

- Avoid eating a heavy meal before practicing.

- Sit on a cushion if you use the floor.

- Choose a relatively quiet and spacious place to sit.

- You may choose to light candles or keep the room dimly lit.

- Stretch out your muscles, especially those in your legs, before and after you sit.

- Wear loose and comfortable clothing.

For a location, choose a comfortable, safe spot. It can be indoors or outdoors, bright or dark. It is important that your meditation spot be quiet and clean, especially when you first begin the practice.

A well-aligned yet relaxed posture plays a major role in the practice of mindfulness meditation. A balanced posture will prevent you from becoming stiff or sore. The following seven points have traditionally been recommended for posture in meditation practice:

- Maintain a straight spine. This not only promotes good health in the long term but also helps you to use your diaphragm properly for breathing. Slouching forward crowds your diaphragm, causing you to begin to breathe using the chest. Leaning back relaxes your diaphragm to the point of uselessness, also causing you to breathe through your chest.

- Place your hands together in your lap, with the thumbs touching slightly.

- Be careful not to bring your shoulders up as you straighten your spine. To help your shoulders relax, let your elbows point slightly outward.

- Lower your chin slightly in order to keep your jaw relaxed. Be careful not to move your neck forward when you do this, since it will result in soreness.

- Keep your eyes fixed on a point. As your eyes move, your mind will move. In contrast, by using a focal point, you will help your mind remain still.

- Part your lips slightly, with your tongue on the roof of your mouth. This helps to reduce salivation and also promotes relaxation of the face.

- Sit comfortably. Ideally, you should sit cross-legged on a cushion. If this is uncomfortable, you can use a chair. You can lie down if this is the only way you can be comfortable, but in this position it can become too easy to fall asleep.

Once your body is comfortably balanced, you can begin to follow your breathing. Count each exhalation silently to yourself. With the first exhalation, say "one" in your mind. With the second exhalation, say "two," and so on. When you first sit down to practice, aim to count twenty-one breaths. If you lose count, it's okay—just start over.

As you count, simply notice your thoughts. Try to name each thought, and then let it go. Notice any sounds in the room. Notice your feelings. Your mind may chatter nonstop throughout the process; this is natural. As thoughts and feelings enter your consciousness, let them come and go as they will.

It is a natural tendency to pass judgment on our thoughts and feelings, to replay old conversations, or plan future activities while meditating. You may also catch yourself indulging in some painful memories or feelings. When this occurs, check your posture and simply pay attention to yourself doing these things. Bring your awareness back to your breath. Notice your judging mind, and let your judgments go. Keep counting your breaths. In time, you will find yourself judging your thoughts and feelings less, even though your mind may still produce a constant stream of chatter and dialogue. Allow yourself to experience your mind rather than engaging in this ever-present mental chatter.

A traditional Tibetan technique helps in understanding and developing this practice. Visualize your mind as a vast clear-blue sky. Your consciousness is the sun shining in the sky. Thoughts, feelings, and distractions pass in the form of clouds in the infinite expanse of the sky. The sun keeps shining, unconditionally, no matter how many clouds roll by. Let the clouds pass. Do not hold on to them. Only count your breath and watch the clouds.

Passive Muscle Relaxation

To help yourself become relaxed prior to mindfulness meditation, you may choose to practice passive muscle relaxation. Lie down in a quiet, comfortable spot. Visualize a clear ball of white light at your feet. The light is soothing, healing, and deeply relaxing. Imagine that the ball comes into your body through your toes. Feel your toes relaxing. Feel the light spread from your toes up through the balls of your feet. Now feel it relaxing your heels and then your ankles. Feel your shins and calves relax. Feel your knees relax. Feel the relaxation spreading up through your thighs. Feel the bones of your legs and feet become deeply relaxed. Now imagine the light relaxing your genitals and pelvis. Feel it relaxing your hips.

Imagine this soothing glow bathing your internal organs, relaxing everything it touches. Feel it relaxing your spine, one vertebra at a time. Feel your nerves relaxing. Feel your belly relaxing. Feel it spreading up through your chest, relaxing your ribs, your heart, and your lungs. Next, imagine this relaxing light coming into your fingertips and thumbs. Feel your hands and then your wrists relaxing. Feel your forearms relax. Feel it spreading through your elbows and up through your arms. Feel the bones of your arms and hands completely relax.

Then imagine this relaxing light spreading throughout your shoulders and neck. Feel it spreading through your jaw, your mouth, and your tongue. Feel your ears relax, your cheeks relax. Feel your nose relax, and then your eyes and eyelids relax. Feel it relaxing your eyebrows, and your forehead. Now imagine this clear light spreading up through the top of your head. Feel your entire head relax.

Your entire body is completely relaxed as it is bathed in radiant, healing, clear light. Spend some time in this state. You may practice mindfulness meditation once you have completed this visualization. (It may be easier to practice passive muscle relaxation using an audio recording of the above script.)

Meditation on an Object

Some people find that they become too distracted when they simply follow their breath and so choose to meditate on an object. This can be any object, as long as it represents something relaxing, compassionate, and peaceful. Many people choose a religious picture or statue. Some people use a candle, although gazing at a flame for extended periods may cause long-term visual damage. Some people choose a flower, or a bowl of water. Some simply choose an item that happens to fall into their field of vision. Focusing on an object is especially helpful in the early stages of mindfulness meditation practice.

Cultivating Mindful Activities

Practicing other forms of mindfulness may be helpful to you if you would like to integrate your meditation practice into other aspects of your life, or if you find that you are unable or unwilling to sit down to meditate.

A variety of other activities can be used to help you cultivate mindfulness skills, provided that you still follow the basic practice of diaphragmatic breathing and try to pay extra attention to your body. In the *Mahasatipatthana Sutta* (Nanamoli and Bodhi 1995), the Buddha himself stated, "Again, a [practitioner] when walking, knows that [they] are walking, when standing, knows that [they] are standing, when lying down, knows that [they] are lying down. In whatever way the body is disposed, [they] know that that is how it is."

What is being emphasized here is not so much the activities of walking, standing, or lying down, but the attention being paid to doing these things. Indeed, when you are engaged in any of your normal activities, you may want to specifically do them *mindfully*. Even though you may not be meditating, everyday tasks can be meditative.

Over the years, people have shared with me several activities that can be particularly well suited to being performed mindfully. These include cooking, painting, gardening, fishing, walking, and eating. The mindful preparation of a salad seems to be very popular. In truth, any routine hobby or task can be done mindfully if you perform it with conscious awareness of your body, mind, and breath.

In order to practice a mindful hobby, break down the activity into its specific parts. Try to be present while performing these parts. Check in with your breath. As your mind wanders, bring it back to the task at hand and the present moment—where are you? What are your hands touching? What do you see? What do you smell? What do you hear? How is your posture?

When you are practicing mindful activities, it is of central importance that you engage all of your senses—sight, sound, touch, smell, and taste—in conscious awareness. You may want to say to yourself, "I am aware of hearing the sound of my feet walking on grass," or "I am aware of the smell of this flower." Combine this awareness with diaphragmatic breathing.

You may take longer to perform the hobby simply because you are more aware of what you are doing. But when you engage in a task or hobby mindfully, you may realize what it is about the task that you enjoy, and why you started doing it in the first place. Mindful daily activities are particularly helpful in cultivating what is called "beginner's mind," the difficult but rejuvenating orientation of freeing yourself of preconceived notions about familiar things.

When to Practice

Taking care of yourself after the loss of a loved one is crucial to your ability to grieve mindfully. When you are suffering the pain of grief, you need to spend some time every day taking care of yourself, including basic activities such as taking a shower, doing the dishes, exercising, cooking, and paying bills. When we are taking care of ourselves, we feel more at ease, and more empowered to live our lives.

Make sure you give structure to your day if you don't have any. Make a daily or even weekly schedule for yourself. Wake up at the same time, and go to bed at the same time. Spend time in the morning getting ready for the day. Plan activities to keep yourself engaged with life, particularly if you want to maximize the suggestions and practices in this book. When we experience great emotional pain, it can be all too easy to become swept away by our intense emotions. A daily schedule of activities will help you stay grounded. Be flexible and forgive yourself if at first you don't keep up with your schedule— it can be very easy to feel guilty if you lapse. Just remember that the purpose of a daily schedule is not to make you feel guilty or ashamed; it is to help nurture a sense of self-worth and balance as you grieve. Over time, you will find yourself relying less on a schedule to take care of yourself.

Initially, however, you'll need to set aside a regular time to practice mindfulness meditation, exercise, and do other self-care activities. In the beginning, you may find yourself practicing meditation whenever the opportunity arises. In time, you may decide to devote a specific time of each day to your practice.

Try to practice mindfulness meditation or a mindful task at least three times a week, for ten to fifteen minutes per session. Eventually, you will be able to practice more often and for longer periods of time, and you will also lose count less often.

The more you practice, the more you will find yourself becoming mindful during other daily activities. This general, ongoing awareness is the ultimate goal of mindfulness meditation.

Keeping Track of Your Mindfulness

Some of the earliest research on meditation found that regular meditators felt lower stress and distress over time, even though the events in their lives remained stressful (see Benson and Goodale 1981). Recent research on mindfulness meditation has shown that it reduces the risk of relapse in people suffering from depression (Teasdale et al. 2000), reduces chronic physical pain (Kabat-Zinn et al. 1997), improves the immune system, and may even alter the hard wiring of our brains so that we are more content (Davidson et al. 2003).

Together with colleagues from the University of Miami (Kumar, Feldman, and Hayes, under review), I have devised a questionnaire that can help you track your progress. You may want to complete this questionnaire every couple of months in order to follow your practice of mindfulness. Please note that List A and List B use different rating systems.

We have found that, in general, people who are experiencing depression have a total score of around 43 (on the questionnaire below) before they start their practice but can increase their total score to around 48 after regular practice. Although this may not seem like a big change, it is quite significant.

List A

1 = almost always   2 = often   3 = sometimes   4 = rarely

1. ___ I try to control how I feel and think.
2. ___ I am preoccupied by the future.
3. ___ I have a hard time concentrating on what I am doing.
4. ___ I try to think about things other than my present situation.
5. ___ I try to escape from unpleasant thoughts when they come into my mind.
6. ___ I am easily distracted.
7. ___ I am preoccupied by the past.
8. ___ I have a hard time accepting some of the thoughts and feelings I have.
9. ___ When I have a feeling, I react to it quickly and automatically.
10. ___ I do things without thinking about the consequences of my actions.
11. ___ I react to most things strongly and quickly.
12. ___ I am easily swayed by my feelings.

_____ = List A Total

List B

1 = rarely   2 = sometimes   3 = often   4 = almost always

13. ___ I focus on the present moment.
14. ___ I try to understand why I feel the way I do.
15. ___ I believe it is okay to be sad or angry.
16. ___ I can usually describe how I feel at the moment in considerable detail.
17. ___ It's easy for me to keep track of my thoughts and feelings.
18. ___ I notice quickly when something is bothering me.

_____ = List B Total

_____ = Grand Total = List A Total + List B Total

What to Expect

Kongtrul Rinpoche has left us valuable advice on the practice of mindfulness:

> Undistracted mindfulness and continuous mental abiding
> may be difficult, and you must proceed by small steps.
> Nevertheless, it is crucial to maintain the effort without
> becoming discouraged.
>
> (Harding and Thrangu 2002)

With repeated practice, over the course of weeks, months, and eventually years, these simple techniques can revolutionize your life. You learn to accept your thoughts and feelings. You learn to trust yourself and your intuition. You begin to learn what we call "radical acceptance," a concept that will be discussed at length later in the book. Most important, you learn to develop, almost automatically, the capacity to endure distress. You increasingly identify with the sun shining above the clouds of your own emotional pain.

Despite an initial honeymoon period, which can last for days, weeks, or even months, when the practice seems to give you immediate returns, you will still have some sessions that are easier than others, even after weeks of practice. I have been practicing mindfulness meditation for more than ten years and still struggle to sit through some sessions.

In both meditation practice and the journey of grief, some days or weeks are easier than others. Allow each meditation session and each moment of life to unfold on its own. There is no set time frame by which to gauge your progress. Expecting yourself to feel a certain way or develop a sense of mastery of meditation after an arbitrary amount of time can easily worsen your tension and distress. It can lead you to judge and worry about yourself, and, as a result, needlessly increase your suffering. Mindfulness can teach you to be patient with yourself, especially when you are in emotional pain and distress.

Remember, you are practicing.

3

The Spiral Staircase

By practicing mindfulness in meditation or as part of other activities, you gradually come to know the recurring nature of certain thoughts and feelings. By allowing yourself to experience your inner dialogue without judgment, you witness how repetitive your mental chatter can be. You may, as many people do, get frustrated by this repetition. And you may feel as though the practice of mindfulness is having little effect on your day-to-day life. However, as you continue to practice, you will begin to notice a change in your inner chatter, and in your attitude toward yourself and others. You will notice flashes of calm in the middle of emotional storms.

This calming effect may manifest itself unexpectedly, such as when you don't lose your temper in an irritating situation. Many of the people to whom I have taught mindfulness report having a changed response to heavy traffic and traffic lights. You may witness a steady change in how you interact with others. Someone who normally annoys you, or with whom you have a difficult relationship, may become tolerable, or even a good friend. You may find that you are more able to tolerate pain, whether it be physical pain, or the pain of grief. You may not be aware of any change until someone else points it out to you.

No matter how the change takes place, it will probably occur gradually. The practice of mindfulness, and how it affects you, teaches us an important lesson about how grief occurs. Cultivating mindfulness, like grief, is not an event but a process, which takes time. Like the practice of mindfulness, grief is gradual, and often repetitious. And in both mindfulness and grief, what you experience in one moment is not necessarily what you will experience in the next.

IMPERMANENCE AND GRIEF

The impermanent nature of life is particularly evident when you experience loss. Your experiences of both mindfulness and grief can remind you of the universality of impermanence, the realization of which is one of the foundations of Buddhism, and an important tenet in most other spiritual teachings. There is a common saying in Tibetan Buddhism: "The conditions for life are few, but the causes of death many." The Indian Buddhist master Nagarjuna talks about how all of our lives are as precarious as a lamp flame in a strong breeze. This way of thinking can remind us of not only the fleeting nature of life but also how precious our life is in its vulnerability to change.

The impermanent nature of life is not limited to our mortality. Impermanence pervades nearly all levels of our existence, from the aging process, to our unending stream of daily mental commentary, to our sometimes fickle and shifting emotions. Like all of these aspects of our lives, grief is also impermanent. The emotional pain of grief fluctuates, changing along with everything around us. Some days can be excruciating in their intensity, and other days may feel relatively "normal."

The Search for Permanence

In the presence of such all-pervading impermanence, we all develop a tendency to seek stability and predictability, sometimes even if it isn't good for us. Stability implies permanence, lack of change. Even positive change can feel threatening and uncomfortable.

We long for permanence in all aspects of our lives, often to the point of missing the present moment. You may yearn for youth long gone, unaware that your life today is what you will see as your youth in the future. You may wish you could reexperience some of your happiest moments, and in so doing prevent yourself from making new ones. You may wish you could stop thinking about someone or something, and thereby lose your experience of today by holding on to an unpleasant feeling. You may even imagine permanence where there is none. All these efforts to seek permanence are, in the end, futile. It is true, but hard to imagine, that in one hundred years, you and everyone you know will not exist.

Emotional Impermanence

When you are experiencing pleasure, you are probably aware that the feeling is temporary, and you may wish that the experience would last longer. You may try to sustain the feeling of pleasure, to hold on to it as long as possible. We all want what is pleasurable to always be easily accessible, and we all would prefer to be permanently happy. However, as Togmey Zangpo wrote in the *Thirty-seven Practices of the Bodhisattva,* the pleasures of this world are as temporary as morning dew on grass—cool and refreshing, but vanishing quickly. Our feelings of pleasure seem to last only an instant and then disappear.

The opposite process occurs when you experience distress, especially when you are depressed. You may tend to assume that you will always feel depressed, and that the causes of your distress are unchanging; you feel powerless. If you have been depressed before, you may find that you tell yourself, "I knew I'd wind up back here." In short, when you are depressed, you assume permanence.

In both pleasure and distress, then, we negotiate different relationships with permanence and impermanence. We often blind ourselves to the present moment by seeking out permanence to our happiness, and by trying to escape the sense of permanence that characterizes our suffering. This unending dance only makes us more vulnerable to the effects of change and can leave us emotionally exhausted. Rather than accept impermanence, we continue the dance, remaining ignorant of life's fleeting nature, and of its lessons for how we should live our lives.

Black-and-white thinking. When we assume that our suffering is stable and permanent, or when we have been suffering for a long time, we begin to engage in what psychologists call black-and-white, or all-or-nothing, thinking. This means we perceive the world through a dualistic eye, seeing things and situations as either all good or all bad. This type of thinking can easily lead you to generalize about your future based on how you feel now. The assumption is that life stinks and it won't get better, and the resulting emotion is, understandably, depression.

In South Asia, there are many tales about Birbal, the advisor to the greatest Mughal emperor, Akbar, who lived about five hundred years ago. Akbar built and consolidated a large empire, throughout what is now India, Pakistan, Afghanistan, and Bangladesh, that was known for its tolerance and prosperity. Birbal was considered the wisest man in the land, and was also known for his quick wit and sense of humor. One tale reveals the antidote to black-and-white thinking.

To test Birbal's wisdom, the emperor Akbar once asked him, "Birbal, what words will always give me counsel, in times of feast and famine, in times of wealth and poverty, and in times of happiness and sorrow? What wisdom do you have for me that will never fail me, and stand the test of time forever?"

Birbal replied, with a smile on his lips, "Your Highness must always remember, 'This too shall pass.'"

What Birbal was actually saying was that when we are tossed about between pleasure and pain, we must remain mindful of impermanence. This type of mindfulness will help you weather the storm of change throughout your entire life. When you are experiencing something pleasant, you will experience it deeper and with greater presence if you know that this pleasure is fleeting. At the same time, remembering Birbal's advice can also help you endure bad feelings. While knowing that pleasure is fleeting can bring you into greater contact with it, knowing that distress is impermanent can give you hope and endurance while you are suffering. Many of us learn this when we exercise, challenging ourselves to tolerate distress if we know there's an end to it. We tell ourselves, "I'm really tired, but maybe if I can just make it to the end of the block . . ."

You may be asking yourself why it's so easy to forget Birbal's advice. The answer is in the tug-of-war between our desire for stability and permanence and our wish for the impermanence of pain. We feel our most uncomfortable and intense emotions as a result of life's unpredictability, and so we seek a sense of permanence, which contributes to a sense of predictability in life. Predictability makes us feel stable, and stability, in turn, gives us an illusory sense of control over the ever-changing landscape of our lives. However, life continues to be, as it has always been, unpredictable, and none of us can really control much of it.

Two Types of Suffering

In Buddhism, experiencing impermanence is known as the suffering of change, which is as inevitable in your life as it is in everyone else's. The suffering of change gives way to unhappiness and uncertainty; you don't know what will happen next. Often, the suffering of change leads to another type of pain, called the suffering of suffering, in which we feel awful when our health, wealth, relationships, and the happiness they bring deteriorates. This type of suffering is recognizable to anyone, since we all experience it sooner or later.

Grief can be understood to be the suffering of suffering experienced as a result of the suffering of change. It is the emotional suffering that comes from the loss of our sense of ourselves and of the world. The suffering can be so intense that you may even stop taking care of yourself. You may eat junk food, begin drinking or using drugs, forget to take prescribed medicine, stop exercising, or become indifferent to your physical and emotional needs. When you experience this suffering for a long time, you stop living in the moment and become stuck in the illusion of the permanence of your suffering. You disempower yourself from hoping for a better way.

In the context of Buddhism, striving for a sense of permanence in this way—trying to hold on to permanence by remaining stuck in time—is contrary to the impermanent nature of reality, and is doomed to fail. In trying to control our suffering, we only increase it. The practice of mindfulness, however, helps us accept the natural law of impermanence, and we become more patient, flexible, and resilient in the face of life's ups and downs.

Mindfulness is the antidote to the powerful pull of all-or-nothing, or black-and-white, thinking. When we assume that our distress will never change, or believe that only joy is worth experiencing, we engage in black-and-white thinking. We spend a great deal of energy trying not to find meaning in or acceptance of what we are feeling, but instead to feel something else. You wind up telling yourself that life seems to be all bad, but that you want it to be all good. Mindfulness reminds us that life is lived in the shades of gray in between.

There is a word of caution to be added here. Some people mistakenly believe that the goal of practicing mindfulness meditation or midnful activities is to become immune to normal human emotions. These people seem to try to stop themselves from feeling. Mindfulness should not make you numb to pain, or indifferent to your happiness or the happiness of others. To be mindful is to allow yourself to feel what you are feeling. You will still get upset, you will still feel joy, you will still experience anger or frustration. What changes is the way you witness these emotions. Your feelings about your feelings soften. You gradually become more patient with yourself and with others, because you are paying attention to the transient nature of your feelings and are more able to accept them.

PERMANENCE AND IDENTITY

The dance of permanence and impermanence is not limited to our feelings. We also assume permanence when it comes to our identities. You have probably spent years developing a coherent sense of who you are. You may define yourself by your skills, your job, your assets, your house, your accomplishments, or your relationships. For example, you may have spent so many years saying, "I am a wife," "I am a husband," "I am a parent," "I am a realtor," "I am a teacher," or "I am a psychologist" that you can't imagine being anything else.

When we think about our identity, we tend to think of it as fairly stable and predictable. We have a relatively fixed set of characteristics and attitudes that we associate with this identity. In many ways, this mental shortcut saves us a lot of time and energy. Living life without an identity would be like going through life without a name. It would be impossible to quickly categorize or refer to yourself or others, and a great deal of effort would be required in order to figure out how you fit in.

However, when we assume a fixed self or identity, we again make the assumption of permanence. There is no part of our lives or selves that is permanent, not even our bodies while we are alive. Scientists now report that we are even physically transient—at this very moment, the atoms in this book are being exchanged with the very atoms in your bones!

We are usually not mindful of the fleeting nature of our existence, this shifting kaleidoscope of thoughts, feelings, and experiences that make up our identity. When you practice mindfulness meditation, you are provided with an opportunity to experience just how impermanent these thoughts and feelings, and therefore your identity, can be.

The nearly-nonstop chatter in all of our minds is the script by which we live our lives. Most of the time, we don't pay attention to this constant chatter. One moment, we are uncomfortable watching our breath; the next moment, we are wondering what is for dinner; and the next we are scolding ourselves for becoming distracted. Mindfulness allows us to focus on this chatter, and to realize how much this constant stream of consciousness affects how we live our lives.

Grief and Identity

We grieve whenever our sense of identity has been shaken. This can happen in many ways—the loss of a relationship, the loss of a home, the questioning of some of our deepest assumptions about our identity, or even a generally positive change such as the birth of a child or grandchild. It is when our identity changes through suffering that we often feel the most distress.

For example, the husband of one of my patients, Lana, suffered a series of debilitating strokes. Over a period of nearly twenty years, he slowly began to lose his ability to walk, talk, and take care of himself. Caregiving became a full-time job for Lana. She stopped meeting with friends and going out to eat, and she gradually withdrew into the demanding and never-ending tasks of caregiving. Her identity became caregiver first, wife and mother second. After her husband died, Lana sank into a deep depression. Her identity was no longer that of a caregiver, but she did not know who she was anymore.

Months later, after narrowly avoiding a car accident, Lana realized that she was still alive. She seized life. She became very involved in her local church and began going out to dinner nearly every night. She soon thrived on meeting new people, making friends, and going to shows and movies. Ironically, her family then began to complain of her apparent indifference toward them. Lana's identity had been transformed, and they did not know who this new person was. Now, after Lana had mourned her husband and reinvested in her own life, her family began to grieve over the loss of the Lana they had become familiar with during the lengthy illness.

We grieve whenever an anchor in our understanding of our identity is lost. Picture your identity as a necklace of precious stones that comes undone and needs to be restrung. If some stones are lost, new ones must be added to replace the old ones. Grief can be understood as the process of picking up the pieces of your identity (the stones) without the help of someone you had assumed would always be there, or without a relationship that was a crucial part of your life (the string). Grief is the process of finding out who you are in a world that is barely recognizable because of the tremendous change that has taken place. You may not be able to answer the question, "Who am I?" for a long time after your loss.

UNDERSTANDING GRIEF

A common concern voiced by grieving people is what they can expect of the grieving process. This is almost an impossible question to answer, since everyone's journey through grief is different. Each grief is as unique as the relationship that was lost, and as unique as your own life. Your history of losses, your family and friends, your beliefs about yourself and the world, and your coping skills all contribute to how you will experience grief.

You may initially approach grief as something to "get over," as if it were a hill to climb. However, grief is more complex than that. Grief challenges our notions of both stability and impermanence—it is always there in some capacity, yet it is always evolving. Grief is also impermanent, but as long as you have an identity, you will experience grief in some way.

Where Grief Goes

In working with grief personally and professionally, I find over and over again that although it is impermanent, grief does not necessarily disappear. The pain and distress of grief lessen, but grief itself changes and blends into your life. Grief becomes woven into the fabric of all of your relationships, and of your understanding of life. Although grief stems from the end or loss of a relationship in some form, it can also be the beginning of a much larger journey—a journey into the very meaning of your life. By understanding how grief unfolds, and how it blends into your life, you can view grief as a powerful teacher.

Grief is a part of life, and, like life, it is unpredictable. Although many people advocate thinking of grief in stages, or phases, which implies a progression from one state to the next, I have not found this way of thinking to be accurate or helpful. Separating a deeply emotional journey like grief into stages implies that there is no going back—that once you pass through a certain stage, you're not supposed to revisit it again.

As I discussed in chapter 1, thinking of grief in phases or stages also implies a sense of predictability, or order. However, I find that grief is often one of the least logical and predictable experiences of life. No one can predict exactly how long grief will last, or how any particular day in the coming year may feel. Grief has many lessons for all of us, and each of them can be learned and relearned, not always predictably.

Coping with Grief

It is very easy to get overwhelmed by how grief feels. However, underlying the painful and distressing emotions of grief is your *ability* to feel. The intensity of your feelings points to the emotional potential that you have in all of your relationships. In other words, the distress of grief is an indication of how deeply you can feel, and how deeply you can feel for someone else. This emotional potential feels particularly overwhelming in grief because the person with whom it would have been shared is gone. For most people in the world, loving someone is the most special task of their life. It would be impossible to engage in this task if you were unable to feel deeply, and this is precisely what grief tells you you are capable of doing.

Understanding Your Feelings

When you are in a relationship with someone, you feel many different emotions each day. Love, anger, happiness, distress, gratitude, and frustration: all of these emotional ups and downs are part of the natural course of being with someone, no matter what the nature of the relationship is. Your feelings may change from one day to the next in both large and small ways. You may love someone intensely, yet be irritated by something he or she does or does not do. You may feel anger one day, and deep love the next. But having these emotions does not guarantee that you won't feel the many emotions in between. We don't say, "I was in the stage of love on Monday," or "I was in the stage of upset on Thursday." We recognize the ups and downs as part of the relationship's constant flow.

Similarly, as you grieve, you may experience many emotional ups and downs. Just as characterizing relationships as having stages or phases usually does not describe how you experience them day to day, thinking about grief as having stages also fails to acknowledge the inevitable emotional ups and downs that characterize it. However, I have found that grief is characterized by periods of intense distress and relative calm that can be referred to as acute and subtle grief.

Acute grief. When you experience acute grief, it is the only thing that you can attend to. It demands all of your attention, and you know that it is grief that is being experienced. It may gradually lose its intensity, but it can still interfere with your ability to do everyday tasks. When you reexperience it, acute grief makes you feel like you have gone back to the days when the loss you suffered was new and completely overwhelming. A lot of the time, feelings of acute grief will remind you just how nonlinear emotions can be; they may not follow a logical or straightforward pattern and may arise as if from nowhere, or for no apparent reason.

I have found that during the process of grieving many people repeatedly reexperience the same intense emotions. Sometimes, these reexperienced feelings, described as "acute grief," can be more intense than they were the first time around. You probably first experienced acute grief at the moment of your loss. Acute grief is the ground zero of grief; it is the reference point of all of your other emotions. Acute grief isn't necessarily marked by sadness or crying. It can feel like anger, anxiety, loneliness, and vulnerability. It can feel like many different emotions all at once, or like one in particular.

Subtle grief. As time goes on, most of your distressing feelings diminish in intensity. This can take months, or it can take years. You may find that some of your feelings linger just under the surface, waiting for an opportunity to present themselves. You may feel like you are waiting for someone or something, or you may feel vaguely upset or distressed. At times, you may also feel as though you can experience happiness and joy again. Over the course of time, you may find that your grieving process is marked more by the blues, or even periods of joy, than the intense emotions of acute grief. These feelings of general distress with islands of happiness, and the time between moments of acute grief, can be described as "subtle grief."

When you experience subtle grief, you are able to go to work and carry on with your life, but you are still grieving. You may not even be aware that you are still experiencing grief; other people may notice, or you may realize it only a little later.

The Spiral Staircase

Acute and subtle grief alternate in a complex dance. This dance is the emotional roller coaster that is the grieving process, and it is what makes grief so unpredictable. When you have experienced subtle grief for a while, you may feel that you have come through the worst of it—and you may indeed be done with the worst of it. However, your hopes may be dashed when you experience intense acute grief again. In order to describe the general emotional path of the grief journey, I have found it helpful to think of grief as unfolding in the shape of a spiral staircase.

Why a Spiral?

Because of how nonlinear the movement between acute and subtle grief can be, I find it is best described as a spiral instead of as a series of steps or a predictable line on a chart. Each circuit of the spiral represents a turning point in your relationship with the loved one you have lost and with your relationship to grief, and is marked by a period or episode of acute grief. These circuits of the spiral are the emotional ups and downs of subtle grief. Each of these twists and turns gradually, sometimes imperceptibly, gets less exaggerated, leaving you feeling better than you did after the last one.

Jackson was a police lieutenant who showed up for a grief support group I cofacilitated. Jackson was very expressive in the group. He sobbed and shook uncontrollably as he talked about holding his dear wife in his arms on their front porch as she died of a ruptured abdominal aneurysm. The pain in his voice was palpable and moving. The group was very supportive.

In time, it was revealed that his wife had died almost a year before, while the other participants had lost their loved ones relatively recently. He had never attended the group because he felt that his sadness was normal. What motivated him to come after nearly a year was that his sadness had returned, just when he thought it was all over. He found solace in knowing that everyone else in the group also had ups and downs. One member of the group, who had lost his wife to suicide more than a year ago, explained to Jackson that grief is like that: wrought with countless ups and downs.

It is particularly helpful to think of grief unfolding in the form of a spiral because spirals are unending and amorphous. They don't form discrete, static shapes like a grid or a square; spirals can always grow. There is no limit to how many loops a spiral can have, or how large it can be.

Spirals are also found in nature—they are the shapes of living systems, such as storms, seashells, and entire galaxies. You can think of your grief as being the spiral of a hurricane. The eye of the storm, the center of the spiral, is the moment of your loss. Each of the feeder bands is heralded by thunderstorms; these are the moments of acute grief, of tremendous emotional pain. In between are periods of calm, periods of subtle grief. Like the grieving process, hurricanes are known for the loss and devastation they bring, but they are also necessary for the life of ecosystems because they open the way for renewal and regeneration.

In the context of grief, this renewal might manifest itself as spiritual, emotional, or interpersonal growth. You may become more understanding of yourself and those around you. Renewal may also mean financial independence or resolution, or a move from one place to another. The gradual movement toward growth and regeneration takes place within the loops of your grief process or spiral. Like the distress of grief, renewal may also happen several times in your grief journey.

The Staircase

With each passing turn of acute grief in the spiral, no matter how many there may be, your relationship with grief and with the loved one you've lost changes. Even though there may be periods of renewal, you will also experience feelings of intense sadness and loss that may seem like setbacks. You may feel as if you are right back where you started. But most likely you are actually making gradual progress up a staircase of growth.

Indeed, most people eventually come to see grief as a period of experiencing intense personal and spiritual growth, like ascending a spiral staircase. You may not always know where the flight of stairs is going emotionally—sometimes you feel better, sometimes worse—but you can know that the whole staircase is your evolutionary journey through grief.

The Unpredictable Course of Grief

Grief does not have an on/off switch. Just as assuming a fixed sense of self can make life easier in some ways, thinking of grief as a structured experience, with a beginning, a middle, and an end, can seem very reassuring. However, just as your identity is impermanent and constantly changing, so is grief. It may feel intense one day and less intense the next, gradually becoming part of your life. The impermanence in our lives will never end—why should grief?

Grief can come and go in its intensity. You may think you're over grief, only to be surprised by the overwhelming feelings of acute grief simply because of a song on the radio, or a dream about a forgotten memory. Many of the people with whom I work have found themselves fleeing from their favorite stores because of something as seemingly innocuous as Muzak. As you grieve, you may feel like a different person as you go about doing familiar things.

The transient nature of grief is one of the characteristics that makes it challenging. It is difficult to tell people who may want to be there for you that you can't know how you will be feeling from one moment to the next. People who aren't experiencing grief have a much easier time being able to predict their moods and feelings because their identities have not been shaken as yours has. Well-meaning friends and family members may wonder why you are feeling the way you are, or why you aren't better, when you may have been better one hour before.

The Labyrinth of Grief

It is easier to think of grief in simplistic, black-and-white terms. It *would* be much easier if once you had experienced acute grief, you moved once and for all into subtle grief, and then the whole affair would be done with. But this is not the case. Grief is not a black-and-white unidirectional progression, but rather, like most other things, has various shades of gray and many ebbs and flows. The spiral staircase of grief can continue upward for a long time, alternating between acute and subtle periods. There is nothing wrong with this process; it is as natural as the movement of the waves on the seashore.

You may find it helpful to think of your grief experience as a journey through a labyrinth. In medieval Europe, many builders of churches and cathedrals created labyrinths on their grounds as places of pilgrimage. The labyrinth was intended to embody the pilgrimage to the Holy Land, which was too far for most Europeans to travel at that time. Labyrinths were also used by Native Americans to represent spiritual quests.

A labyrinth is a complex, winding path, often circular in shape, that you walk. The path usually leads you to a wider, open area in the center that may contain a small garden or a bench for contemplation and rest. Reaching this area is the goal of your spiritual quest. As you walk the path of the labyrinth, you meditate on a problem, or repeat prayers.

The path of a labyrinth is sometimes lined by tall hedges, or it may be very complex so that you cannot see where the path is leading you. Unlike in a maze, which typically contains dead ends, you cannot get lost in a labyrinth as long as you stay on the path. Labyrinth paths weave their way around toward the center, but just when you think you are close to the center of the labyrinth, the path may divert you to its outer reaches. When you are convinced that you are far from the center, the path carries you straight into the heart of the labyrinth, a place of openness and calm.

A labyrinth offers a type of walking meditation. There are many labyrinthine sites around the world used for walking meditations. Circumambulating the Kabbah in Mecca is a walking meditation that is the goal of the Muslim pilgrimage. There is a walking meditation path that travels up each shore of the River Ganges in India, and there is one around Mt. Kailash in western Tibet. Closer to home, Grace Cathedral in San Francisco has a labyrinth open to the public. In addition, farmers will sometimes carve labyrinths into their cornfields, depending on the season.

The spiral staircase of grief is much like a labyrinth. It can be particularly disorienting at first, until its twists and turns become, if not familiar, at least expected. The first year or so of grieving can be disorienting in this way. The next chapter will help you get your bearings. You cannot get lost in the labyrinth of your grief, as long as you stay on the path and remember what Birbal said: "This too shall pass."

4

The First Year

If you were to go on any journey, you would want to plan ahead. You would research the weather so you could bring the appropriate gear. You would investigate the lodging options so you could pick a spot that is comfortable and beautiful. You would try to find out about the place—what to see and do, and how to get around—in advance. You wouldn't want to be unprepared when you arrived, and if you were, you would wish you had known more before you started.

When we begin the journey of grief, however, we rarely have the luxury of planning in advance. There is never a good time for grief to happen, and sometimes there is no warning that it will take place. You often feel overpowered by its demanding, unwelcome, and uninvited presence. Nevertheless, once grieving begins, it is possible to have a general sense of what to anticipate.

This knowledge can be very empowering. However, it is certainly not all-inclusive. We can never know exactly what to expect. Keep in mind that even when you have some advance knowledge grief can still be very unpredictable: you may know what to anticipate in your mind, but your heart may still have quite a few emotional surprises in store for you.

This chapter will help you navigate through the first year of your grief journey. I have found in my work with grieving people that during the first year you will learn what occasions and issues are the easiest and which are the hardest for you to experience. During the first year, you are more likely to experience acute grief, especially in the first few months. You will probably also reexperience acute grief later during the same year. But as time goes on, this acute grief will gradually give way to more periods of subtle grief, and the years will get easier as time goes by.

MEMORIES DURING THE FIRST YEAR

For many people, the entire first year is the most difficult precisely because their memories of the end of the relationship seem stronger than the rest of it, especially during all the special occasions and important dates of that year.

For a while after you experience your loss, you may find it difficult to remember a time when your loved one was healthy or pleasant to be around. Especially if your loved one was afflicted with pain and suffering before the death, you may only be able to remember them this way during the first few months of your grief. If he or she changed emotionally or mentally before death, or acted in strange or even threatening ways, you may find it much easier to recall these difficult moments than to remember more pleasant times. This is a very natural occurrence. It is usually much easier to remember details about recent events than to recall things that happened long ago.

Remembering only suffering or difficult interactions is also a way for your mind to account for the loss of this person's presence in your life today, reminding you of how he or she left you, rather than of the times you enjoyed together. Memories of the end of your relationship that seem to linger for a while are part of the process in which you begin to understand—emotionally, mentally, physically, and spiritually—that this person is gone. These memories help you incorporate the loss of the relationship into the story of your time together. They help you to understand the conclusion of your shared story, and answer the question of why he or she is not with you today.

Eventually, perhaps slowly at first, you will remember other parts of your relationship. Your earliest memories of being together may start to come back to you. You may recall things you enjoyed doing, and time together that you may have even taken for granted. In time, you will remember your relationship as a complete story, with a beginning, and a middle, and not just as a tragic ending.

Being able to recall memories of all of your time together is a critical component of healthy grieving. Once you are able to recall a wider range of memories, you can be sure that you are making progress along the spiral staircase.

Memories Evoked by Your Home

You may have to move to a different home or city, perhaps due to financial, emotional, or interpersonal issues. Moving away from a shared home or town soon after experiencing loss can be one of the most painful parts of the grief journey. Relocating geographically can seem like reliving the loss of a loved one's presence all over again. Moving is particularly emotionally intense because you are leaving behind the backdrop of your shared memories. Staying in the same place, whether it is a house or a city, can allow you to preserve the memory of the person you have lost longer. Where we live is the context of our lives; changing this context adds another layer of awareness of the impermanence of our lives.

Try to be mindful of what your home or city means to you in the context of your loss. What places did you share together? Is there a particular room or part of the home that was special? If you go to these places or parts of the home, watch your breath. You may find yourself feeling anxious at first, taking shallow breaths in your chest. When you notice that you can be mindfully present in these shared places, you will know that you are making progress.

Memories Evoked by Belongings

Even if you don't have to move or relocate after your loss, the act of packing your loved one's belongings can be particularly intense. You may find mementos long forgotten, or indications that your loved one was thinking about you even at the end. In one touching example, a patient of mine found, while packing up her belongings, that her deceased husband had written her a Valentine's Day card, even though he had died in December.

Holding on to your loved one's belongings can preserve their memory. There are widely differing attitudes regarding whether or not it is a good idea to keep the loved one's belongings. Some of the people I have worked with have disposed of their loved one's belongings almost immediately, making every sign of the person's presence—photos, clothes, notes—seem to disappear overnight. Other people hold on to belongings for years. Slippers are placed at the bedside, waiting for someone who is not coming back to put them on, or an extra place at the table is set every night.

Both approaches, and all the possibilities in between, reveal information about where you are in the grief process. Feeling ready to let go of your loved one's possessions can be a sign of movement up the spiral staircase. I would encourage you to not throw everything away, however. After all, this person was an important part of your life. How you deal with the belongings is a personal decision, and one to make at your own pace if possible. The process may happen slowly; perhaps you will first wash the sheets that he or she last slept on, then put away your loved one's shoes, and then his or her clothes.

Try to be mindful of what each decision to either keep something or to dispose of it means to you. Be aware of how you feel about doing so. Also, be mindful of what each belonging means to you, and what it meant to your loved one. Then try to bring this mindful awareness to your own belongings. What would you want done with your things?

UNDERSTANDING GRIEF TRIGGERS

This first year is when the twists and turns of the spiral staircase can feel particularly disorienting. There may not even be much difference between acute and subtle grief at this time—it can all feel pretty acute. This section will help you understand what causes your pain to be particularly intense.

The hardest part of suffering loss is often the moment when you are left alone for the first time. This can be at the moment of separation or death. It can be when your visitors go home, or when your home is empty for the first time. It can be the first time you notice that a familiar voice is absent in your life. It can be when you come back home alone, without your loved one in your life, for the first time.

These first months will pass. The first months and year are the hardest because in addition to your loss being fresh, the form your grief will take is, at this point, uncharted territory. As you begin your journey on the spiral staircase, seemingly random or minor things will sometimes set off a cascade of overwhelming emotions. Other times, you will know months in advance how difficult certain events will be for you without your loved one.

These events, random and otherwise, are your emotional triggers. Triggers are cues in our surroundings that act as mental and emotional signals. They release a set response of thoughts and feelings. When we begin thinking and feeling a certain way in response to a trigger, we feel overpowered by the intensity of the feelings. In the context of grief, triggers are the places, events, people, sounds, smells, and images that remind you of your loss and arouse the feeling of acute grief. When you go to a particular place, hear a certain song, see a particular picture, view a certain Web site, or talk to certain people, you may experience acute grief. For example, seeing an ad for a sale on clothing that you no longer need to buy or doing grocery shopping for one less person can be triggers.

Common Triggers

When you suffer a major loss, your whole world can seem like an almost constant reminder of the absence of your loved one. In addition to people, places, and things, particular holidays and special occasions can also feel overwhelming.

For almost all of the people I have worked with, the most potent triggers are those that remind you of activities you used to share, and celebrations of your life together such as anniversaries. You may find it helpful to make a year-long calendar with room for you to write in. This calendar will help you understand what times of the year might be particularly difficult for you. On the page for each month, write down important dates. You may wish to note the six-month and one-year anniversaries of your loss, dates that were meaningful in your relationship, and any places you would go, or things you would do together to commemorate special occasions. These dates can be when you first met, your first conversation, or your first kiss. The following list of commonly celebrated important dates may help you get started:

Personal milestones

Birthdays

Anniversaries (e.g., of first meeting, wedding, death/funeral)

Beginning or ending of year (e.g., calendar year, school year)

Events and other things related to seasonal changes
(e.g., weather, sports, foods)

Family milestones

Graduations

Weddings

Starting new job or school

Illness or death of loved one

Major secular holidays

Valentine's Day

Mother's Day and Father's Day

Halloween

Thanksgiving

New Year's Eve

Religious holidays

Passover

Ramadan and Eid

Lent and Easter

Wesak

Muharram

Deepawali

Christmas

Hanukkah

This very general list probably includes some dates that are not relevant to your loss, and it probably leaves out major personal milestones. The important thing is that you develop a sense of what was, and what remains, relevant to your particular journey through grief.

These occasions and dates often establish the rhythm of each year in a relationship. After suffering the loss of a loved one, you may find that these occasions scream out their absence. Reminders that an important occasion is approaching can be very subtle and may be things that we normally take for granted. Changes in the weather or length of daylight may quietly herald the arrival of a milestone, or a once-special occasion. Decorations around town or in your neighborhood may signal the approach of a holiday that was your loved one's favorite, or one that you always celebrated together. Seeing particular programs on TV or spending time with out-of-town visitors may remind you that it is a particularly poignant or memory-evoking time of year.

One man with whom I worked, the youngest in a large family from the rural South, taught me how potent holidays can be. After putting up a long, brave fight against the illness, his mother died of cancer in late spring one year. Even though this man lived in a different state from his mother, he had taken on the responsibility of coordinating the medical care between her and her many physicians. Months after her death, he told me that he felt his grieving was complete. Since she had been ill for years before her death, he had had plenty of time to prepare himself during his several trips home. However, because the holiday season was approaching, I cautioned him regarding how he might feel during this time of year.

One day in early December, he called my office to schedule an appointment. When he came in, I could see that he was very distressed. In the past weeks, he said, he had realized just how much he missed spending Thanksgiving with his mother. In the grocery store as he was buying yams, he had become overwhelmed with the realization that she would not be there this year. The music and the decorations in the store, and the fact that he was shopping for a Thanksgiving dinner that she would not cook, all triggered acute grief.

Acute Grief and Its Triggers in the First Year

During the first year and even beyond, acute grief is often triggered by milestones and special occasions. Sometimes, you may find yourself lost in the pain of your grief and not know why. The answer may be in the anniversary or passing of a particularly relevant milestone. Oftentimes, we don't realize what significance these holidays and dates hold for us until we experience loss. This is why having a calendar that has all of your personally relevant holidays and dates noted can be helpful.

Checking the calendar can help you understand and become mindful of why you are feeling a certain way, sometimes in the absence of any obvious triggers. Using a calendar of these milestones can help you to approach milestones and holidays mindfully, empowered from knowing the causes of your acute grief rather than being surprised by the sudden intensity of your own emotions.

You may also experience acute grief when a once-irrelevant holiday or special occasion suddenly has more relevance in the context of your grief. For example, many of the holidays celebrated around the world focus on the issues of birth, death, and rebirth—the cycle of life in the world. Many of our holidays originated as a way for people to honor these natural cycles; fall holidays often acknowledge death or the end of a harvest, and spring holidays acknowledge rebirth, regeneration, and the sowing of seeds. You may experience a tremendous outpouring of acute grief because the themes of certain holidays and special occasions now have greater emotional meaning for you.

COPING WITH YOUR TRIGGERS USING RADICAL ACCEPTANCE

Going through the first year of holidays and milestones without your loved one can be one of the most difficult tasks of your life. Rather than avoiding triggers of acute grief, strive to understand the role that these triggers play, and what roles acute and subtle grief play in your life. As distressing as these triggers can be, it is through them that the task of grieving is accomplished. These triggers mark the turns in the spiral staircase of your grief.

During this first year, you may feel completely alone and vulnerable in the world. You may feel as if you are starting the grief process all over again around each special occasion or milestone. Whenever we are confronted with intense pain and distress, our first reaction is usually to try to run away from it. We continue to try to seek pleasure and avoid pain, even when we are told that our pain is normal—it sure doesn't feel okay, even if it is normal.

But what we do with our pain at this emotionally intense time is very important. If we choose to hide from our pain, we only lie to ourselves. I have found that no matter how hard we try, the pain comes out somehow. If it is blocked off or numbed, we will be blind to why we are feeling the way we feel. One of the people I worked with, Sally, after losing her husband to cancer, found herself acting particularly vicious and mean to her family every evening. When they pointed it out to her, Sally realized that evening was the hardest time of day, since she had to face climbing into an empty bed night after night. Instead of acknowledging her pain, she had channeled it into anger, driving away those closest to her. Once she accepted that underneath her anger was a tremendous amount of pain, it became easier for her to get into bed without losing her temper.

If we turn away from our feelings when we are distressed, like Sally, we risk closing off our hearts to ourselves, and to our relationships. The Buddha's realization that suffering was an inherent part of our existence was not just an intellectual concept; it was a profound emotional event. We were not meant to only feel good; distress is also an integral part of all of our lives. Grief and love are intertwined: feeling the emotional intensity of grief means you can also feel love.

So what do you do with pain as intense as acute grief? You certainly can't run from it, at least not permanently, nor can you dwell in your pain indefinitely. The answer comes from mindfulness: you turn around and embrace the process. This act of embracing is called "radical acceptance."

This form of acceptance is called "radical" because it is completely unconditional. Nothing is turned away; all is welcome. Through radical acceptance, we learn that although mindfulness may change us it does not change the world. You can still experience stress and distress, as well as happiness and pleasure; the world keeps going on as it always has. It is your attitude toward it, and how you approach your distress, that changes. Mindfulness teaches you that there is nowhere to hide from your thoughts and feelings, so you can finally stop running away from them and accept yourself.

The sixth-century Buddhist saint Shantideva (1997) wrote the following in *The Way of the Bodhisattva:*

> To cover all the earth with sheets of hide—
> Where could such amounts of skin be found?
> But simply wrap some leather round your feet,
> And it's as if the whole earth had been covered!
>
> Likewise, we can never take
> And turn aside the outer course of things.
> But only seize and discipline the mind itself,
> And what is there remaining to be curbed?

(5:13–14)

What Shantideva is telling us is that though we may not be able to change our situation or how we feel, mindfulness can help subdue the mind, no matter how distressed or pained it may be.

Although it is a Buddhist concept, radical acceptance has been found by modern psychologists to be a very effective way to deal with many different types of intense, distressing emotions. Psychologists are finding that radical acceptance helps people with drug and alcohol problems to stay sober and withstand intense cravings. It helps people with phobias live fuller lives despite their fears, and it helps people with obsessive-compulsive disorder find healthier ways of acting and reacting to their environment. Radical acceptance teaches that the best way to overcome a perceived threat is not to look for ways to ward it off but to change your relationship to it.

Radical Acceptance and Mindfulness

Acceptance and mindfulness are interconnected ways to change how you relate to distress. The simple act of sitting down to meditate, paying attention to your thoughts and feelings (both pleasant and unpleasant), and paying particular attention to your distractions sows the seeds of radical acceptance. When you practice mindfulness, you simply observe what is happening in your mind, bringing your awareness back to your breath.

There are many different ways that mindfulness teaches you radical acceptance, but they are all grounded in accepting your feelings. When you practice mindfulness meditation or your chosen mindful activity, imagine your mind as a radiant sun, shining unconditionally on the clouds, which are your thoughts and feelings. Focus especially on that which is most uncomfortable: depression, fear, anger, hopelessness. As you count your breaths, remain identified with the light of the sun, allowing each of these uncomfortable emotions to arise.

Guess what? Despite having these disturbing thoughts and feelings, as uncomfortable as they may be, you're still breathing. You're okay. The foundation of mindfulness—following the breath—facilitates your radical acceptance of whatever you are experiencing.

Mindfulness and radical acceptance both require that you have a compassionate and welcoming attitude toward your thoughts and feelings, especially the uglier feelings. When you practice mindfulness and radical acceptance, you are actually giving yourself unconditional love: you are opening yourself up to all of your thoughts and feelings and embracing them all, irrespective of the pleasure or pain they give you.

Even though we may not be able to avoid triggers of acute grief, the radical acceptance we can learn through the practice of mindfulness can dispel some of the suffering of grief. By changing your attitude toward suffering from one of confrontation to one of acceptance, you may in fact diminish your suffering.

Accepting the Person You Have Lost

Radical acceptance also works with regard to how you understand the person you have lost. You may feel that you shouldn't think about your loved one's flaws now that he or she is gone. But we are all imperfect in many ways, and it is okay to think about the imperfections of the person you have lost. Perfection is an unrealistic illusion. It is better to have a realistic relationship to the person you have lost than to try to limit how you feel about him or her. You may feel guilty for thinking about the shortcomings of someone who is dead, or far away. However, by accepting the shortcomings of the person who is no longer with you, you allow yourself to feel the totality of the relationship—imperfections and all. In all aspects of life, relationships based on a realistic understanding of ourselves and our partners are our healthiest and most rewarding.

Distress about Distress

It is common to feel distress about our distress. We feel guilty, sad, angry, or anxious about our sadness, which only snowballs and magnifies the underlying distress. Sadness plus anger, guilt, or anxiety does not equal less sadness; usually it adds up to more suffering for you and those around you. Guilt, sadness, anger, and anxiety: these feelings about feelings are what psychologists call secondary emotional processes. Many times throughout our lives, and especially during periods of grief, it is these secondary emotional processes that complicate and magnify our underlying distress. However, in the face of unconditional love and acceptance, even the most intense secondary emotional process can begin to melt away.

Triggers in the first year set off distress reactions which often lead to a cascade of secondary emotional processes, adding layers of negative emotion on top of distress. By becoming aware of what your triggers are—people, places, things, significant dates, and milestones— you can allow yourself to become mindful and accepting of your distress. This does not mean rushing headlong into your suffering. It means allowing yourself to experience feelings as they arise, mindful of their causes, their impermanence, and your feelings about them. Throughout this book, you will learn many ways to improve your practice of radical acceptance in order to help yourself deal with the emotional triggers of grief and not add to your distress. Knowing that you will meet these triggers and allowing yourself to go through them using radical acceptance is a core method of grieving mindfully.

RELATIONSHIPS DURING THE FIRST YEAR

Triggers can hurt because they highlight the loneliness you feel without the person you were sharing life with. But despite the pain that accompanies them, triggers of acute grief are actually beneficial: they teach us that although grief feels lonely and isolating, it is actually a reminder to us that we are meant to be with people. Grief reminds us of the almost sacred nature of human relationships, how important they are in all of our lives. It is only natural to want to be around people and not want to go through life alone. This is probably one of the main reasons you are reading this book—to figure out what to do with this disturbing feeling of loneliness and separation from your loved one.

When you experience distress, particularly the lonely sadness of grief, it is very easy to isolate yourself and suffer in silence. Many of the people I have worked with found that they retreated into themselves in the first few months after suffering a loss. During this time, you may find it easy to forget the people who care about you. Your grief may feel like a burning coal that would burn anyone who came into contact with it, and you may stay away from others in an effort to spare them from having to experience your burden.

However, because of how important relationships are for all of us, they can often be the best fuel for giving you the endurance to cope with the first year of grief. During the first few months after your loss, you will likely be facing some pretty significant emotional triggers. This is the time when it is absolutely crucial to surround yourself with caring, understanding people.

You may have better insight into some of your relationships at this time—who can best provide an ear to listen to you, and who can best motivate you to get things done. You may also reprioritize many of your relationships because of what you experience in grief, and how you experience it. Many of the people that I have worked with have changed the company they keep as a result of going through the grief process. Similarly, you may find that some of your closest friends are no longer very close to you, or are not very understanding of what you are going through. You may also find that people you had thought of as casual acquaintances are now much closer friends. On the other hand, close friends and relatives may come forward with unwavering support and show you just why you love them.

Shared Relationships

Relationships that you had in common with your now-absent loved one act as emotional bridges to our losses. When milestones approach, you may find that you become more sensitive around those shared relationships. Being around these people can be extremely gratifying and reassuring; however, it can also be particularly challenging.

We often express our darkest, most uncomfortable emotions to those who are closest to us. If you are irritable or reluctant to spend time with some of your shared friends, you must ask yourself why this is the case. It may be that you can more easily direct your grief, and your anger and frustration at the person you lost, toward these people in particular. If these relationships form an emotional bridge to the loved one you have lost, you may unconsciously channel your negative feelings along the bridge and toward those around you, pushing away your shared friends and relatives.

In many instances, it can feel easier, and even more empowering, to sever or break an existing relationship rather than confront your own loss. But moving away from others to deny your own loss is the opposite of radical acceptance, and it can be particularly dangerous. If you try to avoid your own pain by avoiding others, you will eventually find yourself alone. If you find that you are alienating those closest to you, try to bring mindful awareness to how you interact with others. This is one of the hardest tasks we can engage in—to figure out what role we play in difficult or strained relationships, and to be actively mindful in our interactions with others.

Bringing mindfulness into your relationships is a lifelong process. As you work to experience your grief mindfully, you will find that you become more mindful of life in general. You will be able to better accept yourself and the people around you, rather than always being at the mercy of your reactions to yourself and others. You may find that many of your relationships become renewed and invigorated. You can participate in these relationships with greater presence, since you are seeing these interactions as what they are, not as emotional bridges.

KNOWING YOUR LIMITS

It can be easy to misunderstand radical acceptance as wallowing in, or holding on to, your pain. When I ask you to embrace your emotions, it may sound like I am asking you to sit deep inside of depression and give up hope of feeling a different way, or wanting to a feel a different way. As we discussed in the previous chapter, our minds have a tendency to engage in this type of all-or-nothing thinking, of assuming that there can be only pain or only pleasure. Our pain can feel permanent; our pleasure, fleeting. This is especially true when we are distressed. We can easily feel overwhelmed by our pain, and we may assume that it will always be this way. However, it is also when you are feeling completely overwhelmed that radical acceptance works best.

Remembering the truth of impermanence, you can learn to accept how you feel in the moment.

Radical acceptance is an application of what is known in Buddhism as the "Middle Way." This means not plunging headlong into your feelings, but also not running away from them. It means remaining mindful of the impermanent nature of our experiences in order to face our emotional pain. By accepting the impermanence of your emotions and moods, you may find it easier to stay centered, rather than feeling tossed about by the inevitable emotional roller coaster of the first year. Keep in mind that all of your emotional experiences strung together, good and bad, constitute your spiral staircase of grief.

As you practice radical acceptance during the first year, it is important to pace yourself. All too often, I meet with people in my practice who feel burnt out, having spent all of their resources coping with grief very well for a relatively short period of time. However, the spiral staircase has its own timetable. It cannot be rushed or slowed down, and it often seems like it has its own natural life span. Grieving mindfully involves accepting that traveling the spiral staircase is often a marathon, not a sprint. It can be tempting to deny your pain, or overidentify with your pain.

But radical acceptance does *not* mean becoming one with your distress; nor does it mean denying the existence of your pain, or denying the difficulty of coping with it. It does not mean torturing yourself silently, quietly bearing a heavy burden, desperately waiting for it to disappear. If you find it difficult to endure your pain, I encourage you to seek help. This is especially important when you are facing a particularly tough trigger.

If you don't feel that you have adequate support from those around you, I recommend that you seek counseling or join a local bereavement group. If you know now which triggers are the most difficult ones for you to experience, it may be a good idea to mobilize your resources such as healthy coping skills and psychotherapy so you can be prepared for these triggers in the future. Most places of worship and hospitals have regularly held bereavement groups that are full of people like yourself—people who may never have been to a support group but find support in sharing their experiences and intense emotions with each other.

Maintaining an awareness of what to expect as you travel the first loops of your spiral staircase, and using the methods of mindfulness and radical acceptance, you will be empowered to face your first year of grief. As you go through this year, as distressing as it may be, you will begin exploring many of the underlying issues of your loss—what it means to you today, and how you experience the meaning of your life—and receiving priceless life lessons. The next two chapters will help you continue on this path.

5

Closure and Transformation

For most people, the first year of grief can feel like a purely emotional journey. The intense emotions of acute and even subtle grief can feel overpowering at times. During the first year and beyond, life may feel like an endless roller coaster of difficult emotions brought on by triggers such as holidays and milestones passed without your loved one. It may seem that all that you are doing is feeling, and feeling miserable. Establishing closure and recognizing the tremendous transformative capacity of grief can help you understand your experience of loss and attend to your feelings in a healthy way.

UNDERSTANDING HOW YOU GRIEVE

A first step in understanding your loss is to bear in mind that your feelings, however uncomfortable and distressing they may be, are an

essential part of who you are. Feelings, however, don't exist in isolation. As human beings, we tend to do three things nearly simulta-
neously: we think, we feel, and we act, and so every part of you goes
through grief—your thoughts, feelings, actions, and even your body are
all involved in grieving. Consistent with this holistic approach to life,
grief, as psychologists are now learning, is as much a mental and spiritual journey as it is an emotional one.

Even though you may feel like your emotions are all-consuming,
grief also involves important psychological and spiritual work that can
change your life. Engaging in this work mindfully can help you to
transform your grieving into one of the most meaningful tasks you will
ever do. Over the years I have seen many people whose lives have
been dramatically enriched by the decisions they made during their
grief, and by the meaning they found in their experience of grief.

Your feelings of acute and subtle grief, and all of the intricacies
of the spiral staircase, are part of the process of understanding your
loss. The emotional roller coaster that you experience is part of how
we human beings naturally incorporate change into our lives. The
emotions you experience are signals to you that the person you
thought you were, and how you relate to your world, are changing
because of your loss.

The Process of Radical Acceptance

Radical acceptance allows you to mindfully integrate your loss
into your identity. Accepting the fact that you may not know how
you will feel from one day to the next helps limit the amount of distress about distress you experience. Radical acceptance also allows
you to become more at ease with the impermanent nature of all of
your experiences. You accept that your thoughts and emotions are
also impermanent, yet you engage mindfully in their creation and
results.

As we have talked about in earlier chapters, one of the most
natural tendencies that we human beings have is to seek permanence
in an impermanent world. Given this tendency, we may find loss and
change to be confusing and disorienting. But as you go through the
first year of grief, the emotional swings that you experience—the

bewildering twists and turns of the spiral staircase—are actually signs that your loss is being integrated into your sense of who you are and your understanding of the world.

Some psychologists consider integrating the loss to be what "acceptance" is. My work with the bereaved has shown me that acceptance, like grief, is a process, not a finite goal or finish line. Acceptance is not the end of the journey, and its absence is not a sign of failure. Instead, acceptance is something that happens slowly at first, ebbs and flows, and becomes more familiar with each turn of the spiral staircase.

The ups and downs of grief and acceptance are particularly severe when you face emotional triggers. You can make the emotional roller coasters more bearable by finding meaning in both the loss and the grieving process—by finding out what it means to have had your experience, and who you would like to be as you go on this journey.

FINDING MEANING IN GRIEF

I was first introduced to the importance of meaning-making as a college student. One of my psychology professors recommended that I read *Man's Search for Meaning*, written by a remarkable man named Viktor Frankl (1997). Dr. Frankl was a psychotherapist in Vienna when the Nazis came into power. Because he was Jewish, he was sent to a concentration camp. Unlike many millions, he survived the horrors of the death camps. This alone was a tremendous feat. Dr. Frankl attributed his survival, against all odds, to his finding reasons to endure his suffering. Despite the horror of his surroundings—famine, slave labor, disease, unrelenting cruelty, and the constant threat of death—he was able to remind himself of his choice as a human being to find meaning in his life, irrespective of how unbearable that life may have felt.

Some days, he was able to recognize the meaning of his life in a beautiful sunset seen through rows of barbed wire fences and guard posts. Other times, he stayed up at night trying to reconstruct his recently completed manuscript, which had been confiscated and destroyed when he was brought to the camp. When Dr. Frankl was liberated from the concentration camp at the end of the war, he attributed his survival to the realization that we can endure suffering, as long as we have a reason to endure it. Although he could not understand how such cruelty and injustice could exist in the world, he was able to understand what would get him through each day.

Grief Changes Your World

Understanding your loss does not necessarily mean finding all the answers for why it happened, or being able to intellectually explain away your feelings. It does not mean gaining a medical understanding of death, or a clinical understanding of relationships. Understanding your loss means understanding what role the loss plays in your life, and eventually being able to integrate the loss into your identity. It means reconstructing your identity, and your world, after it has been forever changed. Understanding your loss may sound as if it involves thinking a lot about what has happened in the past, but it is really more about deciding how to live your life in the future.

This process often starts before loss has occurred. My experience in working with grieving people is that the seeds of how you come to terms with the loss are planted within the relationship itself. That is, the characteristics and features of your relationship with your loved one determine the questions that come up in that person's absence, and they often shape how you go about answering them.

All of our relationships have certain recurring themes that characterize what each person means in our life. Certain thoughts and feelings, even ways of talking and figures of speech, seem to come up with certain people. For instance, you may know someone you feel you can always talk to when you are in trouble. This may be a particularly healing relationship, one that seems to embody health and well-being. Communicating with this person may feel empowering and validating. On the other hand, another relationship may embody self-destructive tendencies—for example, a friendship with someone who seems to bring out your negativity.

When any relationship ends, you are forced to fill up the space in your life that it once occupied. The role that the person played in your life becomes the focus of your thoughts and feelings. The themes of the relationship may very well become integrated into your grief journey. You may find yourself emotionally disoriented by having certain thoughts and feelings without this person there.

One of the reasons grief can seem particularly intense is the profound psychological changes that are taking place. Your emotions during this time are often a sign that you are trying to find your way in a new world, one that has been changed by your loss. Understanding this new world, and your place in it, is one of the nearly universal challenges of grief.

As you feel your way up the spiral staircase of the first year and beyond, you gradually, and repeatedly, come to terms with what has happened to your life and to your relationship to this world. Like the spiral staircase, this is a nonlinear and lengthy process, and it too has many ups and downs. Being able to engage in this process mindfully can help you to find important life lessons along this journey. Coming to terms with loss mindfully—becoming an active participant in understanding, accepting, and finding meaning in your loss—gives you the power to change your life.

Actively finding meaning in loss is the heart of grieving mindfully.

The "Why's" of Grief

In my clinical practice, I have observed that, at one time or another, most people who have experienced a loss will find themselves asking "why?":

Why have I experienced loss?

Why did this have to happen?

Why am I suffering?

Why does it hurt so much?

You may ask why your relationship ended, why your life has changed, why someone close to you has left, why we die, or why we suffer. You may ask why the person you have lost did what they did, or why you didn't do something differently. You may be asking what point there is to life, what it all means, and why we are here. These questions arise frequently in the midst of acute grief, when there often seems to be no explanation to justify the existence of such pain.

My experience has been that these questions are best answered personally instead of universally. That is, it is more important for you to find *your* answers to these questions, on *your* terms, rather than try to figure out the meaning of life and loss for everyone. Even if you have come to terms with loss before, each relationship is unique. There may be new avenues for you to explore, or new facets to discover. The meaning that you find in this particular experience of grief may emerge from something unexpected, forgotten, or new.

The answers to the riddle of your suffering—why you are experiencing it, what will get you through it, and how you will grow because of it—may also unfold over time. That is, over time you will probably find several answers to each of your "why's," instead of just one. Sometimes, even these answers may seem inadequate. This is okay. It is best to allow yourself to accept different meanings as they arise, since each turn of the spiral staircase may bring with it new explanations for both the presence of suffering and how to endure it.

By now, it should be clear to you that there are no easy answers for why you are experiencing loss and what it all means within the scope of your life. In fact, human beings have been asking these same questions for thousands of years, through religion, science, and philosophy. These are humanity's attempts to explain life's basic mystery— why we, and all the things we experience, are subject to change, loss, and decay.

The Death of the Buddha

From a Buddhist perspective, there is no mystery to loss. It is simply a universal reality. As the Buddha lay dying, he told his disciples, "Everything that has a beginning has an end." What he was really saying is that loss is universal. When we look closely at our ordinary, everyday existence, we see that nothing is static; therefore, loss and change are inherent in our lives. The Buddha was pointing out that every facet of our existence (even our identities, as we discussed in chapter 2) is impermanent and so it is subject to loss, grief, and sorrow.

Sand Mandalas

To bring home the impermanent nature of everything in our lives, Tibetan Buddhist monks create complex artistic creations out of colored sand and then destroy them. *Mandalas* (Sanskrit for "circle") are colorful designs that can symbolize different things—the human body, divine realms, or meditational deities. They can symbolize specific aspects of the body, images for visualization, or entire universes. In Tibetan Buddhist rituals, monks painstakingly assemble mandalas, arranging sand, grain by grain, in intricate, symmetrical designs. As the monks make a mandala, lamas present spiritual teachings about specific meditational practices related to that mandala. After a few days, while chanting solemnly, the monks sweep up the mandala into a pile of jumbled colored sand, which is then offered to a river or the sea. The intricate universe of the mandala disappears and dissolves into a mixture of colored particles, leaving behind no trace of the design. What was once an elaborate representation of the complexity and potential of our lives becomes a lesson in impermanence.

In many ways, these mandalas symbolize what happens to all of our relationships and experiences, and ultimately to all of our lives. No matter how intricate, complex, or beautiful they are, all of our experiences are temporary. There is nothing that exists that we cannot cherish and therefore grieve when it is lost. In the practice of mindfulness and mindful activities, even each exhalation can teach us how universal loss and change are. Each breath that we exhale is an ending, which is followed quickly by a new inhalation—a new beginning—and the cycle repeats over and over again. Our lives depend on the cycle of loss and regeneration that is evident in our very breath.

TWO TYPES OF LOSS

There are two general types of losses that you can experience in your life. In the pages that follow, we will discuss the questions and feelings that come up in connection with these two types of loss.

Sudden Loss

The first of these types of loss is sudden, unexpected loss. This occurs when in an otherwise happy relationship, one partner decides to leave, or when a loved one dies in a sudden accident or violent event such as murder or suicide.

In these instances, it can be very difficult to find meaning in the loss itself. Since there was no shared good-bye, no anticipation of the end of the relationship, it can feel more like a shocking theft than a loss. Not having a chance to say good-bye can make it hard to believe that the relationship has ended, and to imagine that any reason or meaning can be found in the loss.

Even though it may be difficult to find meaning in the loss itself, you may still be able to find meaning in your grief—your response to the loss. For example, you may create meaning by advocating for change so that others won't have to experience what you went through. When my wife and I had our son, we attended a hospital-sponsored baby-care class with other new parents. The nurse leading the class stressed the importance of not shaking babies and passed out pamphlets explaining the risks and dangers of shaking a baby, as part of a new public awareness campaign. She told us that a baby had suffered brain damage and then died because of excessive shaking, and the baby's grandmother had responded to this tragic death by working to alert the public to this danger. She gave meaning to the death of her own grandchild by trying to make sure that other babies wouldn't also die, and that other families wouldn't suffer as she was suffering.

The Unanswered Questions of Sudden Loss

If your loss was sudden, such as a loss resulting from suicide, murder, or an accident, you may spend a long time struggling to understand why it happened, without finding any complete answers. Especially in the case of suicide and murder, it is impossible to ever completely know someone else's motives, or what your loved one experienced during the event. The people involved might not have even understood the situation clearly themselves. Part of what makes this type of loss so tragic and intense for those left behind is precisely this not knowing; the particular devastation is how unfinished the relationship feels. The exact details of the loss remain forever shrouded in mystery, and they may become complicated by lawsuits and intrusive media coverage. As a result, the relationship can seem even more unfinished.

Unexpected losses often seem as if they could have been avoided. For this reason, it is completely natural for you to want to know why the loss occurred the way it did. You ask yourself, What if someone had walked into the room? What if someone had said something different? What if they had taken a different street? What if they had left the house later? The reality of the loss itself can become eclipsed by an endless series of "what if's."

There will probably never be sufficient answers to the "what if's." There is only the inescapable reality of the loss. Since we can never truly know the feelings or perspective of anyone else, it is important to remain mindful of your own thoughts and feelings. Because you may never know what your loved one experienced, it is especially important for you to understand what this experience means to you. Your own thoughts, feelings, and meaning are the only knowns in the uncertain landscape of sudden, unexpected loss.

Gradual Loss

The second type of loss is slow, gradual loss. This is what happens when you are in an unhappy relationship and you and your partner finally agree that you must part ways, or when someone you love is diagnosed with a life-threatening disease like metastatic cancer or Alzheimer's disease. In these instances, loss is expected. There are usually many good-byes along the way: a last meal in a favorite restaurant, a last visit with friends together, a last night in the same bed, maybe even a last coherent conversation.

This type of loss, by virtue of its gradual nature, allows for more communication with your loved one along the way. Much of the work of understanding the loss may have taken place before the loss itself, during the period of anticipatory grief. However, gradual loss can still strike at the heart of your assumptions about life and who you are.

When loss is gradual, your mind and your world have enough time to slowly change and adapt to the idea of losing your loved one. Before your loss you may have found yourself alternately stepping back and moving closer to your loved one as your relationship ended. On the other hand, you may have found yourself cherishing each and every moment with your loved one, becoming inseparable for as long as you could. Some days you may have been able to make plans for a future without your loved one, acknowledging that he or she would not be there; other days you may have found that contemplating a future without your loved one was like staring at a gaping black hole.

As you experienced the early phases of gradual loss, the awareness that this time together was fleeting, and the realization that this relationship was ending, guided your behavior and your feelings. Even if this realization was not conscious, it may have been hovering in the background. The process of dismantling the world you shared with your loved one, even if you were unable to knowingly envision life without them, began during the period of anticipated loss.

For people experiencing all types of loss, expected or unexpected, emotional and mental hardship are the hallmarks of grief. Having time to prepare, as is the case with gradual loss, does not necessarily make grief any easier. The answer to all of your "why's" may seem elusive and obscured because of your intense emotions. Any hope of sorting out what has happened to you may seem unrealistic in the face of your distress.

I often find that people who experience sudden loss wish they had experienced gradual loss, and many people who experience gradual loss wish they had experienced sudden loss. In either instance, it is often not possible to completely recognize that the person you have lost is no longer physically in your life. Finding closure can help facilitate this recognition.

FINDING CLOSURE

The term *closure* is often misunderstood. Many people erroneously view closure as sealing off from their hearts and minds the remembrance of a relationship, or having the ability to never think about the person again. But for many people, finding a sense of closure actually allows the search for meaning in grief to begin.

When casual friendships or relationships dissolve, closure can mean talking together to find out how the relationship failed. It can mean giving back the other person's belongings, or reclaiming yours. These tasks allow you to move forward, and to see completion, real or symbolic, in the relationship. In these instances, closure is the feeling that you have both said good-bye.

When death occurs, closure can be much more difficult because there is no possibility of exchanging belongings or talking things through. Death is beyond our control; loss occurs whether we are ready or not, and we are forced to come to terms with it. In the face of death, closure is often an outward recognition of intense, inner loss. Finding closure after the death of a loved one does not mean forgetting about the relationship, or denying your feelings for the deceased. Closure means feeling as though you had a chance to say good-bye, even if this was not actually possible.

Closure in Sudden Loss

Unexpected losses, such as those that result from suicide, murder, accidental death, or sudden physical or emotional distance, can prevent us from saying good-bye to our loved ones. It is important in these instances to find a way to say good-bye, in order to allow for closure of the relationship and the unfolding of your grief. When a face-to-face conversation was impossible, it is especially important to find a way to feel that you were able to say good-bye emotionally and spiritually. You can do this by performing a ritual to acknowledge the end of the relationship. This symbolic farewell can take the form of a wake or a commemoration ceremony—either among friends and family, or privately. For many of us who work with the terminally ill, holding a yearly collective remembrance event allows us to contemplate all the people who have died during the year to whom we were unable to say our final farewells.

However, just as a face-to-face good-bye does not necessarily insulate you from the intensity of grief, a commemoration ritual may not make the pain go away either. What it does permit is a mental, emotional, and spiritual acknowledgement that loss has happened. It allows you to acknowledge the immense task ahead of you, even if you were not present for the final moments of your loved one's presence.

There are many ways to carry out a symbolic farewell after sudden loss. The father of one of my patients had a sudden heart attack while she was out at a movie, and he had died by the time she rushed home from the theater. In order to say good-bye to him, she wrote him a letter, which she carried to his favorite beach and cast into the ocean. This simple ritual allowed her to feel connected to her father one last time, just long enough to acknowledge his death. Many of my patients have lit candles and incense at a specially designated time or place to facilitate a sense of "good-bye." Someone I know even went on a pilgrimage to her husband's ancestral home in Ireland after he was killed in car accident. She wore his wedding ring as a pendant in order to bring him with her for this final trip home.

Use your creativity and your intimate knowledge of what was special to your loved one to say good-bye in a symbolic way. This may mean writing a letter or taking a trip, as in the above examples, or something else. It may mean going to a special place, or doing a ritual at home. What is important is that the action allows your feelings to be expressed.

The Five Things

Dr. Ira Byock, a pioneer in the American hospice movement, has talked extensively about "the five things" (1997)—the topics that typically need to be covered in order to facilitate closure. I encourage people to articulate these five things to their dying loved ones, and also for their loved ones to articulate them. These five things cover all of the emotional territory of any relationship and may be discussed over days and months durings its natural course. When you are mindful of the finitude of your days together, you may see what a luxury it is to be able to consciously have this type of conversation.

As you read over these five things, try to recall instances when you were able to talk to your loved one about these themes, even when there was no intention of the communication being final.

Recalling yourself saying any of these five things can help you to feel that the relationship was able to achieve a natural closure on some level. If you weren't able to actually address these topics, because of the circumstances of the relationship or the type of loss, you can have this conversation symbolically, such as in the form of a letter, visualization, or artwork.

The five things may be hard to say if you are idealizing your relationship. In many ways, saying the five things makes the loved one you've lost human again, instead of a focus of reverence or hatred. If any of these five things is difficult to express, it may indicate that issues related to that particular theme are standing in the way of your ability to find closure.

The five things are:

1. *I'm sorry.* Everyone in a close relationship has some regrets. None of us is perfect, especially the way we treat each other. Apologies are often spoken long before remorse is felt; out of a sense of duty, we may say "I'm sorry" long before we feel it. All apologies, whether big or small, hasty or well planned, pave the way for forgiveness. If you were not able to apologize for something you regret, you may find some comfort in symbolically and intentionally asking for forgiveness now.

2. *I forgive you.* This can be forgiveness about anything and everything. Forgiveness can be thought of as radical acceptance toward someone else. Forgiveness is not to be confused with forgetting. However, when you forgive, through the power of compassion, you release the hold that this issue has had on your life. Rather than feeling unresolved outrage or a sense of justice unserved, you take upon yourself the responsibility for living life on your terms.

3. *I love you.* Love is why you are grieving. Love transcends all sorrow, but sorrow can be fueled by love. Asking forgiveness and forgiving wrongs opens your heart to the full power of love. Acknowledging this love is an

affirmation of the relationship, your grief, and your capacity to share yourself with another human being.

4. *Thank you.* What did you learn from this relationship? What was special about your time together? How did your life change as a result of your loved one's presence, or even loss? Perhaps you learned to love deeper than you had thought possible, or perhaps you learned how to change the oil in your car. This is what you can thank your loved one for.

5. *Good-bye.* There is hardly ever a right time to say good-bye. If you have already lost your loved one, saying good-bye after their loss is a recognition of his or her absence, your grief, and your having cherished his or her presence. Saying good-bye to someone who is already gone does not dismiss that person from your life, or mean that your grief is over. Remember, grief does not end, even though it may stop hurting. Grief only changes.

Taking time to say the five things, out loud, in your mind, or on paper, allows you to develop a sense of closure in your shared relationship—a closure that comes from expressing your feelings, both good and bad, toward your loved one. Even if you feel that your loved one cannot hear you, it is important to be able to articulate and express for *yourself* these five things. Ideally, the five things can be brought into your current relationships as well.

SETTING THE STAGE FOR PERSONAL TRANSFORMATION

As painful as grief can be, each round of triggers offers an opportunity to reexamine yourself, your relationships, and your world. With each turn of the spiral staircase you encounter potent reminders of life without your loved one. Experiencing these reminders mindfully allows you to move toward closure and acceptance of how your world has changed.

Every journey up the spiral staircase of grief is unique. We may not know how long this spiral journey will take. Approaching grief as a life-changing event can help you shift your outlook from one of wanting to rush through it to one of accepting each day for what it is: emotionally, mentally, and spiritually unpredictable. This is a crucial part of radical acceptance.

Acceptance of loss is a gradual and constructive process that begins with closure. It happens whenever you allow yourself to experience all of the twists and turns of the spiral staircase. Remember, acceptance is a path, not a goal. With each turn of the spiral staircase, you find a new aspect of your relationship to the world, and a new standing in it without your loved one. Acceptance facilitates the reconstruction of meaning. When you seek meaning for or an understanding of what you are experiencing, you actively reconstruct your world to accommodate the changes you have experienced and continue to go through. The empowerment that comes from realizing just how active a role you play in the construction of your world is the vehicle for harnessing the transformative power of grief.

The renowned grief psychologist Robert Niemeyer (1997) describes this potential for reconstruction as an indicator of how grief is indeed an active process in which we play an important role. Even though we may feel as if grief is something that has been forced upon us, or to which we are being subjected, it is actually something in which we actively participate. Our whole world changes when we grieve. Undergoing this process mindfully allows us to engage in the transformation consciously.

Becoming mindful of this transformative capacity of grief is one of the most meaningful and powerful ways to understand your loss. Because you may never know precisely why, when, or how a particular loss took place, using your loss as a life-affirming and transformative event can help you to shift your focus from "why me?" and "what if?" to the here and now.

Guidelines for the Transformation of Grief

In order to guide the process of transformation, you need to know exactly what you understand about your loss, and what drives your understanding. Through observing many, many people go through the grieving process, I have developed some general guidelines for facilitating transformation in acute and subtle grief:

First, when you are experiencing acute grief, your main task is simply to feel. Keep in mind the importance and impermanence of grief. Remember, this is the time for radical acceptance, in which there is no denying or hiding from the pain of loss. By practicing mindfulness meditation or other mindful activities, you can improve your ability to weather the storm of acute grief. Make sure that your decisions are motivated not by your desire to shield yourself from vulnerability, but rather by an appreciation of how precious relationships can be.

Second, when you are in the relative calm of subtle grief, become mindful of the times when you feel the healthiest—the most alive, at peace, or fulfilled. Which healthy activities or relationships bring you the greatest meaning and joy? Are there particular people or activities that make you feel more in touch with the direction you want for your life? If you are feeling lonely or isolated, what is holding you back from meeting people? What kind of people would you like to spend time with? Is there a healthy way of living that you have been putting off?

Finally, when you are experiencing subtle grief, think about any unfinished business or promises you may have made to the person you have lost. Were these promises healthy? If they were, have you been able to fulfill your end of the deal?

As you can see, most of the decision and meaning making takes place during subtle grief. Although subtle grief is less intense than acute grief, it is still an emotionally charged time. Using the opportunity for reflection offered by the relatively less intense feelings of subtle grief helps you to open yourself up to your emotions and harness their power to transform your life. If you do not allow yourself to feel their intensity, then there will be nothing to harness.

The next chapter will help you explore how to achieve personal transformation through loss and how to face typical challenges along the way.

6

The Transformative
Search for Meaning
in Grief

Many of the world's spiritual traditions value, and even hold as a central tenet of their teachings, an appreciation of the preciousness of life. The Tibetan Buddhists teach that the foundation of all spiritual endeavors is the realization that we must treasure and respect life as a human being. The emotional intensity of grief often adds a sense of urgency to this realization. This is perhaps the most positive potential meaning of your grief: the deep understanding that your own life is subject to profound change, and that this vulnerability is reason enough to embark on your own spiritual evolution. As the Buddha lay dying, he said, "Everything that has a beginning has an end," and then, "Strive untiringly for your own enlightenment." The realization of the connection between impermanence and spiritual evolution was the last teaching of the Buddha.

For many of the people that I have worked with, this realization has resulted in their changing jobs, moving to a different part of the country, severing dysfunctional relationships, or intensifying healthier ones. I have seen people deepen their spiritual practices, correct past mistakes, find forgiveness for old wrongs, and come to terms with addictions. In these instances, the questions asked regarding grief change from "Why did it happen?" to "What is holding me back from fully actualizing my purpose in life?"

MINDFUL MEANING MAKING

The search for meaning in your experience of loss can help you to endure the intense emotions of grief. Viktor Frankl made an important discovery when he was interned in concentration camps: that we, as human beings, can bear immense suffering and emotional pain as long as we have a reason for doing so. By finding a reason, or meaning in your loss, you can then find meaning in the emotional suffering of your loss. In the pages that follow we will develop an understanding of how mindfulness can help you to find meaning in your grief, and how the search for meaning can help you handle what may feel like a vacant hole in your chest.

Mindfulness gives you a safe space in which you can feel what you are feeling without judgment, criticism, or conditions. By practicing mindfulness meditation and mindful activities, you build a trusting relationship between yourself, your thoughts, and your emotions. This self-trust is essential for being able to ride out the twists and turns of the spiral staircase, paying attention to all thoughts, all feelings, no matter how pleasant or unpleasant. By allowing thoughts and feelings to come and go, and merely witnessing their ebb and flow, you begin to become familiar with and trusting of your capacity to feel, rather than attached to a certain way of thinking or feeling. By engaging regularly in this practice, you lay the foundation for your ability to tolerate the intense distress of acute grief and find meaning in the pain.

Spiritual Meaning Making

In the context of mindful grieving, emotional pain, as uncomfortable and distressing as it can be, provides an opportunity for personal spiritual growth—your emotional, mental, and interpersonal movement toward who you want to be. For many people, spiritual growth means developing a closer relationship to God, or a higher power, or acting on core spiritual beliefs. However, spiritual growth can also be a secular journey toward self-realization, toward being the best person you can be. Spiritual growth is an inherently creative process, in that it requires new perspectives on what may seem to be familiar situations. Mindfulness facilitates spiritual growth since it helps you to develop a welcoming and open attitude toward life. Both mindfulness and spiritual growth help you cultivate acceptance, forgiveness, and compassion toward yourself and others.

There are many Buddhist teachings that ask us to reflect on how much time we waste in idle pursuits. For example, how many hours of television do you watch? How many hours have you lost mindlessly surfing the Internet or playing video games? When you use your time this way, do you feel better afterward? Does engaging in life by mindlessly passing precious moments help you to grieve better? What if you devoted a fraction of this time to your own spiritual development? Pleasure and pain always come and go; they are impermanent. Personal growth and self-actualization stay with you for the rest of your life.

Pleasure, Pain, and Equanimity

In Buddhism, life as a human being is considered the most precious vehicle for spiritual growth. However, we often miss opportunities for growth, distracted from our potential by our endless pursuits of pleasure and retreats from pain. This wild-goose chase usually stops only when we are faced with the sense of helplessness that accompanies extreme distress. Most of the time, we feel entitled to pleasure, but experiencing pleasure also usually feels insufficient; you always still want more. It is only when we are distressed that we say, "Enough!"

Distress motivates you to want to feel *better*, instead of *more*. The world's spiritual traditions all seem to equate this sense of feeling better with feeling a connection to others. When you behave with respect for yourself and those around you, you feel more in harmony with your environment. Distress inherently feels unharmonious; you usually want to reach out to others, or feel soothed by a comforting friend, to restore your sense of belonging and connection.

Your distress may be fueled further by the loss of this special person or special relationship. With your loss comes a sense of being out of harmony with your world; the landscape of your life has been permanently altered. The profound distress that accompanies grief has the potential to show us the futility of our pleasures, and the misery of our pain. In Buddhism, this sense of futility and helplessness is actually encouraged, because this is the seed of equanimity—calm, peaceful acceptance of what *is*, rather than attraction to pleasure or aversion to distress; accepting what we enjoy, but being mindful of impermanence; accepting our emotional pain, but not being consumed by it.

Radical acceptance is a path, whereas equanimity is a goal. Equanimity can have a tremendous impact on how you live your life and relate to those around you. Equanimity in our relationships means that we can reconnect with the compassion and acceptance that comes from realizing the impermanence of all of our relationships.

According to Buddhist thought, the phenomenal amount of emotional, mental, and behavioral energy we spend running after pleasure and away from pain distracts us from the ability to live in equanimity. When you become consumed by your distress, or lose yourself in the intoxicating buzz of pleasure, you lose sight of the precious moments that make up your life. You also lose sight of the spiritual potential that could be actualized by redirecting your emotional energy toward cultivating a mindfully aware life.

Mindfulness is the antidote to this universal, nearly constant bouncing back and forth between attraction to pleasure and aversion to pain. When you practice mindfulness, you don't lose or deny your ability to feel. Instead, you learn to accept whatever emotional reality is in front of you, without sadness about sadness, without anxiety about anxiety, without anger about anger. When you react to distress with distress, the result is twice as much distress. In a state of mindfulness, when you feel unavoidable distress, you accept it, and when you feel pleasure, you accept it.

Equanimity During Hardship

This emotional acceptance without judgment forms one of the main foundations of the spiritual path in Buddhism. Buddhism has a long tradition of accepting hardships in order to train the mind to appreciate what simply *is*, rather than allowing it to seek comfort and ease. This does not mean romanticizing distress, however, or wallowing in misery and discomfort. Nor does it mean identifying only with your psychological wounds and scars, or practicing some sort of spiritual masochism. The following example may better demonstrate the concept of equanimity.

The Buddha taught his monks to go forth every morning to beg for their daily meals. At that time in India, it was generally assumed that wandering monks would eat only particular vegetarian foods. However, the Buddha and his monks would eat whatever was offered to them, making no distinction between a desirable and undesirable meal, or between vegetarian and nonvegetarian food. Every time they ate, the Buddha's monks would practice radical acceptance by eating whatever was put in their begging bowls.

Usually, families would offer the monks whatever they happened to be cooking. Families who sought blessings would prepare delicious meals for the monks' pleasure. Other people would test them, putting in rotting meat one day, exquisite meals another. Someone even put coins into one monk's bowl, and he ate them! Whatever was given to the monks was accepted quietly and graciously. For the monks, the act of begging for food was an opportunity to practice mindfulness of attraction to pleasure and aversion to displeasure. Each meal was a lesson in equanimity.

For most of us, hardships and other opportunities to practice equanimity come along naturally and need not be sought after with each meal. When these hardships arise, they can be accepted as opportunities for growth and mindful practice, much like the monks accepted their meals.

The Courageous Path of Radical Acceptance

The acceptance of emotional hardship is the core of radical acceptance—simply being present with your feelings in the here and now, rather than longing for something different. Radical acceptance provides you with shelter from the stormy emotions of grief—sadness, anxiety, anger, helplessness, and guilt.

The example of the monks eating anything they were given is an example of passive radical acceptance of hardship—it requires others to act in order to make it possible to practice mindful awareness. In this instance, food is simply received. Practicing radical acceptance when you are faced with suffering is considerably more active—it requires your awareness and presence, and all the work is done by you. For this reason, radical acceptance, especially during grief, is a courageous way to approach your feelings.

Courage and Fear

It is important to remember that emotional courage arises from a very natural human fear of distress, emotional pain, and being alone with loss. It is often fueled by the fear of encountering suffering in your life. We all have it. It is almost instinctual and, as a child learns not to touch a hot stove, we only need to go through emotional pain once before learning that it is something to fear. However, courage relies on fear. Without fear, there is no courage, only foolhardiness. Emotional courage is not something that is easily recognized by others; no plaques or trophies are awarded for enduring emotional pain. Instead, this is a quiet kind of bravery. All that is required for emotional courage is to be present when you are suffering.

Often our first inclination when faced with the suffering of someone else or even ourselves is to turn away, to block or numb the experience in some way. You may make a passing joke, ignore it, or rationalize and justify it away. To a certain extent, these are natural ways of coping with distress. However, if you numb yourself to your own distress, if you continue to hide under the covers of denial or addiction, or if you wallow in or glorify your pain, you slowly weaken your capacity to feel. You become numb to the reality of your feelings, and the feelings of those around you.

Lessons from Equanimity and Radical Acceptance

In order to not feel distress you would need to stop feeling everything. This is the lesson of practicing equanimity—pleasure and pain actually have a lot in common. They are the two sides of the coin of our ability to feel. To deny ourselves the ability to feel grief or to avoid the emotions of grief would be to erode the essence of our wonderful human capacity for deep, intimate love.

Similarly, when you wallow in your misery, when your identity is your suffering, and your suffering becomes your identity, you weaken the capacity to move away from pain and into healing. Although suffering may be painful, it becomes so familiar that you wouldn't know what to do with yourself if you did heal. Your suffering and you become one, and you slowly forget your capacity to feel good, or to make meaning from your pain.

In either instance—turning away from suffering or holding on to it tightly—the healthy expression of emotion is blocked. Mindful grieving asks that you observe these tendencies, with the goal of simply allowing yourself to feel what you are feeling without imposing expectations or judgment. These feelings are the fuel of your spiritual growth in grief.

THE ALCHEMY OF GRIEF

Alchemy was an ancient philosophical and scientific tradition practiced in the European Middle Ages and Renaissance. To uninitiated observers, the alchemists seemed to be concerned with how to transform base metals, such as lead, into more valuable metals, such as gold. Although they were seemingly involved in a purely materialistic pursuit, the alchemists were also concerned with a profound spiritual process—how to transform coarse experiences, such as distress, suffering, and ignorance, into meaningful and sublime experiences, such as compassion, transcendence, and self-actualization. The renowned psychologist Carl Jung was influenced by alchemical texts as he developed many of his ideas about self-actualization.

The alchemists, like Buddhists, learned that spiritual evolution is not given to us. Instead, like pure gold, it must be mined and distilled from our everyday experiences. For example, it is not usually moments of comfort and ease that cause us to ask deep questions about life or explore our spiritual potentials. These questions usually arise when our world is shaken during periods of intense pain and distress. The pain and distress are the metaphorical lead and mercury that the alchemists sought to transform into spiritual gold.

Reconstructing Your Future Self

One of the things that gives us a sense of having a fixed, stable identity is the feeling that we know where we will be from one day to the next. In any relationship, there are expectations about future plans, which may be specific, such as plans to go to a certain place for a vacation, or abstract, like growing old together. In any case, these expectations about the future constitute what can be called a "future self"—an expected identity, one that you hope will be realized.

One of the reasons grief can feel disorienting is that when your loved one dies or leaves, this future self becomes unraveled; all the plans you made together are now impossible. As days pass—days you had hoped to share with your loved one—your loneliness may be all the more apparent.

Awareness of the unconscious tendency to project yourself into the future allows you to intentionally set healthy and positive goals for yourself, so that you can work to become the kind of person you want to be. Because a future self is lost along with the departed loved one, many people come to realize that the future self and the present self are the same person—who you will be tomorrow is a result of who you are today. Consequently, finding meaning in your pain involves asking yourself who you want to be as a result of your grief.

Because it is one of the most emotionally intense experiences that human beings can have, grief can be disorienting. Your day-to-day life is drastically and unmistakably changed by loss. Your future life is uncertain. A veil of distress shrouds your past. However, grief provides a valuable opportunity for reorienting yourself in the manner you see fit. I have seen many people use the pain and distress of grief like skilled alchemists. Although overwhelmed at times by the pain of loss and separation from their loved one, they find, after the fact, that they are able to grow from their suffering. That is, they realize, months after they began feeling better, that their grief, though painful, has changed their lives for the better.

Unconditional Self-Acceptance

The transformation of distress into spiritual or even psychological growth is by no means limited to the world's spiritual traditions. The psychologist Carl Rogers (1995) wrote that feelings are a combination of emotions and the meanings we assign to them. In Rogers's view, being fully present with feelings—cultivating mindfulness toward our feelings—is an almost universally applicable medicine, because he firmly believed that feelings allow us to share our most intimate and vulnerable aspects with others and ourselves, leading to the healing of emotional pain. Even when pain continues, Rogers believed, accepting the hardship and challenge of emotional pain is the act of accepting yourself unconditionally, not just when you are feeling good.

For Rogers, unconditional love and self-acceptance was the challenge in all of our relationships, presenting endless opportunities for relieving pain, isolation, and distress. From his perspective, how you approach your feelings is how you approach the world. Unconditional self-acceptance, then, means unconditional acceptance of others—an orientation toward forging relationships, seeking connection with others, and welcoming others without criticism or conditions.

Relating to the emotions of your grief with unconditional love and self-acceptance is the cornerstone of the process of building the life you want to live tomorrow. By allowing, accepting, and embracing your feelings as an indivisible part of yourself, according to Rogers, you move closer to self-actualization. This is the essence of transforming grief into spiritual growth.

In this context, your emotions are signals of your capacity to connect with your own ability to feel for yourself and others. Your feelings during grief are telling you about your capacity to love, share yourself, and be with another human being despite the universal vulnerability and impermanence of all your relationships.

The Mystery of Suffering

Emotional pain, especially during grief, is one of the emotions that defines us as human. Grief has been with the human species as long as we have been able to sustain relationships. The emotional pain you feel after loss is a vivid illustration of the close relationship between grief and love. Like a metal that is transformed through alchemy, grief is the transformation of feeling love into feeling loss. It is neither punishment nor weakness.

This transformation is the mystery of suffering—that being in pain ourselves can cause us to increase our love and compassion for others. When you suffer, you tend to reach for others with an urgency and a vulnerability that are usually rarely shown. When you suffer the pain of grief, you are in close contact with the most tender part of your heart—that part of you that loves others. When we talk of the pain of grief, we are really talking about a deep sense of compassion for yourself and for those around you. You may even notice that your prayers have particular potency when you are suffering the most. For this reason, the suffering of grief has within it a potential for profound appreciation of life and relationships.

The mystery of suffering is one that all of the world's religions and spiritual traditions attempt to address, although there are no simple answers offered in any of these traditions. As you know, leading a virtuous life does not guarantee anyone a future of comfort and ease, free from loss and pain. Similarly, feeling intense distress now may not be a consequence of past reckless or unkind behavior, nor does it provide a shield from experiencing loss again.

Why Do We Suffer?

Finding meaning in the pain of your grief begs the central question: What are your assumptions about suffering? Do you consider suffering to be a punishment, or is it simply a part of life? If pain is not universal, why you have been singled out? Does it mean you're a bad person? Does it mean failure, or weakness?

These questions are all variations of "why?" and your asking them can be understood as an attempt to find meaning in your pain. Looking deeper, we see that they actually point to the underlying assumptions about yourself as a person. The questions you ask yourself about your pain reveal how you view distress in particular, and emotions in general, in your life.

I frequently meet people who think that their experience of loss and emotional pain is a punishment from God, or the result of "bad karma." Some people feel that the intensity of their pain means that they have been singled out, even though grief is universal. Other people feel abandoned by God, without hope or any higher purpose to their existence.

There is simply no way to verify any of your interpretations about why any specific loss you experience occurs the way it does, or why it feels as intense as it does. It may help you to remember that people tend to interpret grief and distress as punishment when their self-worth is low, or when the loss was particularly tragic or sudden. Recall that the meaning you give to your loss has more to do with how you live today than with the details of how it happened. Your loss is probably not punish*ment*, even though it can feel punish*ing*.

OBSTACLES TO TRANSFORMATION

In grief, pain is the mirror of love—it is because of a connection to another being that you suffer pain due to that person's absence. It is *not* a sign of weakness, or fragility, but a sign of one's courage to open up to another human being. The pain of loss is the potential for affinity and an indication of the preciousness of the human connection.

Often, periods of acute grief are too intense to allow you to focus on issues of spiritual growth. Just as in the previous chapter I recommended using the time of subtle grief to explore issues related to your grief, I again recommend using times of subtle grief to explore the transformative, spiritual potential of the emotions you feel during acute grief. Again, your main task in acute grief is simply to feel, with radical acceptance, what you are feeling.

During periods of subtle grief, reflect on how you cope with the intense feelings of acute grief. Do you feel that you are able to grow in some way from acute grief? If not, your growth may be blocked by obstacles. Some common obstacles to the transformative potential of grief are discussed below.

Stagnant Relationships

While working with the bereaved I have often witnessed that when someone is experiencing grief, others may find it difficult to appreciate the grieving person's realization of the impermanence of human existence. Your very presence may remind some people of the fragility of their own existence and relationships. They may be interested in making you feel better only so they do not have to witness your pain. Or, they may find that the changes that you are undergoing upset the comfortable but maybe unhealthy patterns in your relationship. On the other hand, your grief journey may result in changes that deepen an existing relationship.

I have found that those relationships in which grief is accepted are usually those that also empower spiritual growth and well-being. These relationships tend to be dynamic and flexible, and they encourage genuineness and self-exploration.

Addiction

If you have a problem with addiction—to drugs, alcohol, sex, shopping, or even ways of expressing yourself, such as anger and depression—grief can bring about unique challenges. In my work with people wrestling with addiction during grief, I have found that the temporary relief that comes from satisfying addictive cravings is not "free." It comes at a high emotional price. The distress that is suppressed by the addictive behavior seems to ferment, growing more potent under the surface of each numb day. Like a limb that has fallen asleep, when the emotions of grief come back to life after the numbness of addictive behavior has worn off, they are much more intense.

Cravings will usually surface during acute grief, and if you act on these cravings, it is usually before acute grief has naturally subsided. What you miss is the natural transition from acute grief to subtle grief. Consequently, if you cope with your grief by relying upon addictive behaviors, it is very likely that you will mostly experience interrupted acute grief.

It is all too easy to get caught in an intensifying spiral of pain by oscillating between numbness and acute grief. In these instances, you may be feeding your addiction by not acknowledging your pain, and by not experiencing subtle grief. Addiction disempowers your inherent ability to develop equanimity; you run from pain to numbness with ever-increasing severity and urgency. Your moments of lucidity are fragmented and characterized by chaos and acute pain.

It is of absolute importance that you use your experience of emotional pain to overcome your addiction. This may be the central task of your grief, and it may also be the ultimate meaning of your loss. Whatever challenges and opportunities grief and suffering hold for you will go unanswered if an addiction is perpetuated during grief. Much of the work in this book is impossible to do if your pain is being masked by addictive behavior. Your grief may just be the best opportunity you will ever receive to overcome the power of your addiction and cultivate your own inner power. The presence of grief provides you an opportunity to learn how to feel again. By practicing mindfulness in conjunction with rehabilitation, therapy, groups, and so on to overcome your addiction, you free yourself to live your life.

Guilt and Self-Blame

Guilt is often part of the cluster of emotions that characterize depression. In grief, guilt may also be fed by unfinished business in the relationship. When you feel guilty, you become absorbed in your own pain and your own low self-worth. Guilt does not easily allow for change. When feelings of guilt dominate your experience of grief, they become obstacles to your spiritual and personal growth. The relationship between pain and love becomes obscured and the potential for spiritual growth during grief becomes eclipsed by self-doubt, self-loathing, and self-blame.

Guilt makes it very difficult to seek spiritual solace and growth. To further complicate matters, guilt is almost always self-perpetuating. Most of us know that excessive guilt is not healthy, so we may even feel guilty about our guilt, and then we feel even worse about ourselves for allowing this cycle of guilt to take place.

Filled with self-blame, you may feel that life is miserable because it includes such suffering and that you have no potential for growth or spiritual development because you aren't worthy enough for such lofty goals. If you are finding yourself feeling guilty for something that happened in your relationship, review the five things in chapter 5. What do you need to be forgiven for?

When you experience low self-worth or guilt during your grief, you probably feel a sense of deserving punishment, misery, and pain. If you have a connection to a spiritual tradition or practice, you may feel as if you are being punished by God, or as if your spiritual beliefs are no longer meaningful. It is extremely important for you to explore your understanding of spirituality at this time. If you believe in God, is your God angry and punishing? Or is God a compassionate being who tries to soothe your pain? If you feel that your spiritual beliefs are not helping you anymore, do you need to explore them in greater depth and detail?

Often, coming to terms with the emotions of your grief involves reevaluating your spiritual life in order to accommodate what you are experiencing. Before we experience loss and suffering, we tend to take our beliefs for granted. When we suffer, we may suddenly feel that they are inadequate. When we are shaken out of our everyday experience by intense emotions, we have an opportunity to rededicate ourselves to spiritual practice, and to come to terms with our lives, our relationships, and our experience of the world. This is the invitation that grief offers—the possibility to transform and realize your spiritual potential.

7

Grief and Depression

The idea that grief can be experienced as a spiritually transformative task is the central premise of this book. However, as creative and life affirming as this task is, it is never easy, nor does it often feel very pleasant or enjoyable. This is very hard work, mainly because of the emotional intensity that comes with grief. As we discussed in chapter 6, in addition to grief's common emotions such as sadness and anger, you may also be experiencing other hallmarks of distress—feelings of guilt, hopelessness, and low self-worth. You may even find yourself wondering if life is worth living.

For many people, these disturbing thoughts and intense feelings are obstacles not only to transforming grief but also to living in general and can often seem like depression. Indeed, for up to 35 percent of people who experience grief, this emotional intensity becomes an episode of depression (Zisook et al. 1994). During the grief journey, depression may start around the time of important milestones, or be triggered by an episode of acute grief. The purpose of this chapter is to help you figure out whether you are experiencing depression and, if so, how to treat it so you can get on with the task of spiritual transformation.

UNDERSTANDING MAJOR DEPRESSION

I have found that many people who suffer from clinical depression, also called *major depression*, see this condition as a sign of defeat or weakness, something to be ashamed of. But it actually takes a tremendous amount of strength and courage to go through depression, even though these qualities are precisely the ones many depressed people believe that they are lacking. There is no shame or weakness in being depressed, even though depression can make you feel this way. Depression is an experience that some people have while moving up the spiral staircase, and they may need some assistance in order to continue the journey.

If you suspect that you are depressed, be mindful of your thoughts and feelings as you read this chapter. Many of your reactions to what you learn—shame, guilt, hopelessness, helplessness, withdrawal—may in fact themselves be part of your depression. Also, know that if you are depressed, you may have to read this chapter several times before you absorb the information it offers.

Most important, remember Birbal's message: this too shall pass.

Diagnostic Categories

Although grief can often seem like depression, there are subtle differences between the two. In my work as a psychologist, I am frequently faced with the task of untangling these subtle threads in order to understand what a person is experiencing. To help you sort out the two in your own life, below I have detailed the diagnostic criteria that I use in my practice.

Bereavement versus Major Depression

In order to differentiate between grief and depression, psychologists use *The Diagnostic and Statistical Manual of Mental Disorders,* fourth edition *(DSM-IV)* (American Psychiatric Association 1994). According to the *DSM-IV,* bereavement is the reaction to the death of a loved one. Even though bereavement can feel like depression, a diagnosis of major depression is not usually given until at least two months after a loss. After two months, you may be diagnosed as having major depression instead of bereavement.

Before the end of the two-month period, however, you may be diagnosed with major depression if you have certain symptoms: 1) feelings of guilt that are unrelated to things you did or did not do at the time of death, such as medical decisions you had to make; 2) certain types of thoughts about death; 3) preoccupation with worthlessness; 4) extreme fatigue to the point of not being able to do your normal activities; 5) inability to do your normal, day-to-day activities for a long period of time, or not being able to do them nearly as well as you used to; or 6) hallucinating things other than your loved one.

Two months after your loss, the diagnostic criteria for major depression involve having specific feelings during the same two-week period that are different from how you usually feel. A diagnosis of major depression requires that you have at least five of the following symptoms, including the first two: 1) depressed mood, reported by you or other people; 2) a significant decrease in interest or pleasure in almost all of your activities during most of the day, nearly every day; 3) significant weight loss or weight gain without any effort on your part, or increased or decreased appetite; 4) difficulty falling asleep or sleeping too much; 5) too much or too little activity, observed by other people; 6) fatigue or low energy nearly every day; 7) feeling worthless, or feeling excessive or inappropriate guilt nearly every day; 8) decreased concentration or ability to think, or being indecisive nearly every day; and 9) recurrent thoughts of death or suicide, attempts to commit suicide, or having a plan for suicide.

In addition to having at least five of the above symptoms, people diagnosed with major depression more than two months after their loss must also have these symptoms most of the day nearly every day for at least two weeks, and the symptoms must cause significant distress or impairment of normal functioning. If these symptoms are caused by a drug or medical condition, or if they occur within two months of the death of a loved one, they are not categorized as major depression.

Who Gets Depressed?

Even though you may feel being depressed means that there's something uniquely bad about you, or that you are not as resilient or strong as other people, major depression is the most common mental-health problem. It is estimated that in the United States, one in four people will experience depression in their lifetime. This means that probably more people will experience depression than high blood pressure. Clearly, depression is a serious problem that many people face. In addition, those who have experienced major depression before are more likely to experience it again. However, new research, discussed at greater length later in this chapter, suggests that the practice of mindfulness meditation can reduce the risk of relapse.

In my experience, when people are more depressed than grieving, they feel more hopeless about themselves and the future. They have a quality of apparent absolute helplessness, to the point that they become isolated or alienated from friends and family members, that is particular to depression more than grief. The most alarming symptom of depression is often suicidal thoughts and impulses. If you find that you are having suicidal thoughts, seek help immediately from a qualified mental-health professional.

The Mental Side of Depression

The experience of depression usually seems overwhelmingly emotional. However, as in grief, you may also go through a lot of changes in how you think and experience the world. You may wind up trying to avoid what is hurting you or reminds you of your feelings. Or you may find yourself constantly ruminating about your thoughts, your feelings, and your loss.

Many psychologists now appreciate that depression may affect your underlying assumptions about yourself, the world, and the future, and that it is also affected by these underlying assumptions. These assumptions usually stem from beliefs that have little or no basis in reality, and they arise automatically, almost unconsciously.

Your underlying assumptions about life can be better understood as patterns. They do not manifest themselves as a single thought; instead, they are part of a collection of thoughts, feelings, and resulting behaviors. Frequently, these assumptions take the form of a self-defeating internal dialogue, such as "I can't cope with this," "It's all my fault," "I am doomed in every relationship I have", or "I deserve to hurt."

These unconscious underlying assumptions seem to happen on their own, and they can become so integrated into your identity and your relationship to the world that they seem to have always been a part of you. You may believe that you have always felt this way, and that your world has always been as you see it now, through the distorting lens of depression. Gradually, though, these assumptions, generated unconsciously as a result of depression, change how you behave and how you treat others.

The Role of Schemas

These automatic thoughts and behaviors perpetuate the emotions of depression and, in turn, are perpetuated by them. They form the filtering eyes and ears of depression, allowing only input from the world that will help to keep you depressed, biasing your experience of life. The psychologist Aaron Beck has referred to this tendency toward bias as a cognitive schema—a template by which you experience and perpetuate your reality, your thoughts, and your mood. The schemas, or underlying assumptions that are a part of depression, form a vicious cycle of negative emotions.

Schemas don't always perpetuate negative emotions, and in fact they save us a lot of mental energy. We simply would not be able to function without them. One of the first schemas we develop is called "object permanence." As babies, we learn that when a blanket covers our toys, they have not magically disappeared but are simply hidden. We quickly adapt to this knowledge, and stop expending energy looking elsewhere for what we are seeking. We learn to realize when something is out of our view it's not gone forever but will instead come back. Not having schemas at all would be just as much of a problem as using schemas that perpetuate depression, low self-worth, or self-defeating behavior.

The driving forces of harmful schemas tend to be automatic thoughts that are inaccurate or predominantly negative. I find that we tend to use negative, self-defeating automatic thoughts more when we are distressed—anxious, depressed, or angry—about life, or about something that has happened to us. When you enter a particularly intense emotional journey like grief, you may, without realizing it, use these negative automatic thoughts more often, particularly during periods of acute grief.

As you read about the different types of automatic thought patterns in the pages that follow, try to think of specific instances when you have used them, and note these on a piece of paper.

All-or-Nothing Thinking

When you engage in all-or-nothing thinking, there are no shades of gray, only black-and-white. All-or-nothing thinking permeates most other automatic thought patterns. When you engage in all-or-nothing thinking, experiences, relationships, and even you are categorized as "all good" or "all bad." And in depression, you don't often find yourself thinking of much as "all good." Usually, reality and life are perceived and felt as being "all bad," full of suffering and misery. Many people specifically think of grief this way—as something entirely bad, from which nothing good can result. If you make this assumption, you are sending yourself the erroneous message that there is no transformative potential in grief, and that the only result of grief is suffering.

I have found that after experiencing loss, people often use all-or-nothing thinking when remembering their loved one. You may forget the day-to-day irritations that this person caused, and how difficult your relationship was at times. Or you may forget the reason you loved this person, if you are thinking of him or her as all bad. You may perceive one of you as all good, and the other as all bad. You forget the complexity of your loved one and your relationship. You forget that most relationships occur not in black and white, but in shades of gray. When this happens, all-or-nothing thinking results in strong feelings of guilt or anger.

One of my patients, Leona, was left destitute when her husband died. During the course of their retirement, they had managed to spend almost all of their money on expensive vacations and risky investments. Soon, Leona was evicted from her apartment after failing to pay rent for several months. She became consumed by her anger at her husband. He became the source of all of her frustrations; she even blamed him for bad traffic.

One day, I asked her about how they had met and fallen in love. By the end of the session, she had realized how much fun they had had together, and how their financial choices had been mutual decisions. They had in fact talked many times about their dwindling finances, but they had decided together to live life together to the fullest, and she recognized that it was not all his fault. After this session, she found herself back in touch with her love for him. Only then was she able to move forward in her grief.

Selective Abstraction

When you focus on one detail in a relationship or interaction, and this detail takes over your entire experience, you are engaging in selective abstraction. For example, one of my patients, Julio, came to a session distraught. He reported having felt on edge for the past week, afraid that he was about to be fired from his job at a law firm, despite being a conscientious and dutiful employee. He explained that one of his colleagues had taken his usual parking spot. Julio assumed that this was a sign that he was no longer welcome at the firm. At our next session, Julio didn't bring up his job. When I asked him what had become of his fears discussed in our last session, Julio told me he had learned that this particular colleague had a habit of taking other people's parking spots. In a way, he was now one of the "in crowd," because he had suffered the same hassle as everyone else at the firm. Julio's baseless assumption that he would be fired resulted from selective abstraction.

As you grieve, you may find it helpful to reflect mindfully on the memories you have of your loved one. Are you assuming something about your relationship without evidence? Are you doubting whether your love was real, now that the relationship is over? If so, the filter of selective abstraction may be obscuring a clearer and more realistic perception of your relationship.

Overgeneralization

When you draw broad conclusions about yourself, other people, or the world based on one incident, you engage in overgeneralization.

One of my first patients, Don, had been through a bitter divorce five years earlier. He had married his high-school sweetheart right after their college graduation, but after six years of marriage they had grown apart. Don had learned that his wife had cheated on him toward the end of their marriage, and he swore never to become romantically involved again.

Five years had passed, and he had not dated anyone. He now sought therapy because he felt that, at the age of thirty-two, he should be trying to meet women. In our therapy, we discovered that whenever he met a woman he was interested in he assumed that she too would cheat on him. He would then immediately lose interest and would sabotage any chance at pursuing the relationship. In time, after much work, Don was able to trust women again. When I last saw him, he was happily involved in a long-term relationship.

It is common to engage in some overgeneralization after the end of a difficult relationship. Often, people who have just broken up with a partner will say to themselves, "Men are no good," or "Women are impossible to get along with." Some degree of overgeneralization is a normal, temporary response to loss. A problem arises when you become convinced of these thoughts and begin living your life according to them.

Arbitrary Inference

When you have a fixed idea about the world or a relationship, either without proof or despite proof to the contrary, you engage in arbitrary inference. This frequently happens in depression, and especially in grief. Almost all of the grieving people I have worked with have at some point told me that they have no friends, and that their family isn't there for them anymore. On further inquiry, I often find that they have been receiving numerous phone calls, letters, and e-mails from friends and family, but that they haven't responded to any of them. Often, making an arbitrary inference means letting your negative emotions—sadness, isolation, hopelessness, and so on—distort your experience of the world. You wind up telling yourself that you are depressed or alone for a reason, even if the reason does not really exist.

One of my patients, Bill, became depressed some months after the sudden death of one of his family members. Bill had suffered from depression before, when he was first starting his career as an actor. One week, Bill, now an established actor, came into the session doubtful of his acting ability, convinced that he was unable to act despite having received numerous glowing reviews in the local paper. It turned out that earlier in the week, during a rehearsal, a fellow actor who was also a close friend had corrected one of his lines in the middle of a scene. Bill had been corrected, as have all actors, many times during his career; it was nothing new. What was new about this situation was Bill's depression, which relied upon a schema that told him he was no good at his work. Bill made an arbitrary inference from one casual correction, allowing it to eclipse his recognized talent and even his friendship with this fellow actor.

Magnification and Minimization

When you overvalue the relevance and consequences of distressing events, and when you undervalue the relevance and consequence of positive events, you engage in magnification and minimization. When you view as catastropic something seemingly minor, like getting cut off in traffic, or a family member being a little late for an appointment, you engage in magnification. When you keep yourself in a destructive relationship, in which you must constantly brush off critical and disparaging comments or even abuse from someone else, you engage in minimization.

One of my patients, dating for the first time after a lengthy and bitter divorce, became devastated when her new boyfriend did not call her back the day after they had gone out to dinner. She jumped to the negative conclusion that he was no longer interested in her. But a week later she told me that he had had a family emergency and had surprised her at work with flowers three days after their date. Had she continued to magnify the relevance of his not calling, she likely would have sabotaged the relationship herself. Another of my patients became depressed because she felt isolated. When I asked her about her daily schedule, I found that she actually had a packed social calendar every week. She was habitually minimizing the value of her interactions with friends. Magnification and minimization keep you from seeing the world in front of you as it really is.

Personalization

When you assume responsibility for negative events that have nothing to do with you, you engage in personalization. This process is quite familiar to most parents. When a child does poorly in school or has trouble with sports, for example, parents frequently blame themselves. Depression often intensifies this tendency to self-blame. When you are depressed, you may even feel guilty or responsible for events taking place thousands of miles away.

One of my patients, Jerry, had been driving the car when a drunk driver ran a traffic light, killing his wife. More than a year after her death, even though he knew her death was not his fault, this feeling of guilt kept plaguing him. We gradually discovered that his ongoing feelings of guilt were triggered by his routine of reading the entire newspaper every morning, which he almost always ended by reading the obituary section. He felt a personal sense of guilt every time he read about someone dying in a car accident, which happened often. He became more depressed after reading or hearing about fatal car accidents because of his unconscious tendency to personalize these events. Eventually, once he was able to avoid reading about car accidents for a few months, Jerry stopped personalizing every traffic fatality he heard or read about.

Treatment of Depression

Although we have talked a great deal about the mental processes that contribute to depression, depression is not purely a mental problem. There can be many different reasons why people become depressed. As I have already mentioned, having experienced depression before increases your chances of experiencing it again. You may also be at increased risk due to your genes; if your family members suffer from depression or other mental-health problems, there is a higher chance that you will also. Additionally, hormonal changes can bring about depression, as can problems in how your thyroid gland or pancreas functions. Before you consider treatment choices, consult with your physician to rule out these or other medical causes.

If you feel that you are depressed, it is important that you make decisions about how to get help that you feel comfortable with. Treatments these days tend to emphasize a multipronged approach. That is, there may very well be several causes for depression, not just one, and successful treatment will require addressing these multiple causes, possibly using different methods of healing. If you find that your mood is not changing no matter how hard you try, it is important to seek help or try a different method.

Psychotherapy

If you feel that you would benefit from therapy, find a therapist you feel comfortable with. Frequently, word of mouth can be the best way to find a good therapist—ask friends, family, or a trusted healthcare provider. What exactly defines a good therapist? The right therapist for you is someone who has the proper training and credentials, experience with the problem you are dealing with, and, most important, someone with whom you feel at ease and able to express yourself openly. Research over the years has shown repeatedly that the degree of comfort and warmth you feel from your therapist can be just as important, if not more so, than what he or she actually tells you (See Summers and Barber 2003).

There are many different theoretical orientations taken by therapists: cognitive behavioral, existential, humanistic, psychoanalytical, interpersonal, eclectic, integrative, and so on. Extensive research has been done on cognitive behavioral techniques, and this modality tends to be the most strongly supported empirically; therapists of different orientations may also utilize cognitive behavioral techniques. However, in my opinion, no particular theoretical orientation is necessarily the right one. Instead, what is more important is that you feel that the approach has a good fit with your own personality and beliefs. What matters most is how you feel about your therapist, that you understand what he or she tells you, and that you participate actively in the process.

Antidepressants

Many people have strong objections to using antidepressants, or any psychiatric medication, until they find themselves feeling helpless in the face of depression or overwhelming anxiety. I usually bring up the use of an antidepressant when someone has been in a state of profound despair and is having a hard time finding reasons to live, or when someone feels unable to control thoughts of hurting or killing him- or herself. For many of these people, the use of an antidepressant during the course of therapy is extremely helpful. At first, many patients feel ashamed, as if they have failed, when they begin using these medicines. In time, they realize that there is no shame or failure in exercising treatment choices that can help their mood and their quality of life.

Research on the use of antidepressants versus psychotherapy has been fairly consistent for the past thirty years. Researchers continue to find that psychotherapy administered together with antidepressants is more effective than either talk therapy or medication alone, especially for relapse prevention. If a particular antidepressant worked for you in the past, it may be helpful for you to take this medicine again now. If you have never taken an antidepressant before, remember that there are many different types—if one does not suit you, another one may. These medications should always be taken under the supervision of a physician or qualified mental-health practitioner.

Many of my patients who take antidepressants tell me that these medicines do not make them artificially happy as much as take away the sharp edge of depression. Contrary to popular myth, antidepressants don't make you walk around with a permanent grin; instead they can give you the space and energy with which to overcome depression.

Diet and Exercise

When you feel depressed, you tend to eat depressed. You gravitate toward high-carbohydrate, fatty, salty, and sugary foods. You may eat when you are not hungry, or you may not even eat at all. Additionally, the sluggishness that usually accompanies depression can make the very thought of getting exercise seem exhausting. Because of neurochemical changes that can take place in depression, it may literally physically hurt to exercise.

Poor diet and little exercise are an often-overlooked component of depression. I find that lifestyle choices—diet, exercise, and meditation—can be extremely important in promoting and maintaining a healthy outlook and state of being. Recent research also shows that a healthy diet and exercise routine can reduce the severity of depression, in addition to simply enhancing your physical health. The food you eat can send a profound message to your body and your sense of self-worth—are you worth taking care of? Are you worth mass-produced drive-through food, or a wholesome sit-down meal?

After a significant loss, people often go through profound dietary changes. It can seem pointless to cook for just one person, or one less person. It can also feel very strange to show up at your favorite restaurant without the person who usually accompanied you. But however your eating routine changes, it is still important for you to take care of your body with proper nutrition.

Similarly, the idea of exercising after a loss can be particularly draining. If you had an exercise routine before, keeping up with it may feel unrealistic. Judging from the experiences of my patients, though, returning to an exercise schedule almost automatically helps us to feel better. Exercise and mindfulness go hand in hand, in that they both draw your awareness back to your breath, and to your body. Now that you have some mindfulness skills, you may find that they help you exercise more effectively. If you did not exercise before your loss, consult your physician prior to beginning a routine. As long as you have your physician's okay, this is a great time to begin taking care of yourself.

MINDFULNESS AND DEPRESSION

One of the best tools developed to challenge unhealthy automatic patterns of thought, and ultimately defeat the underlying assumptions that they support, is the practice of mindfulness meditation. Recent research suggests that mindfulness meditation is particularly potent in reducing the risk of relapse associated with major depression (Segal, Williams, and Teasdale 2002). That is, once you have had major depression, you can actually reduce your risk of having it again with the practice of mindfulness meditation.

Mindfulness and Automatic Thoughts

Mindfulness meditation can reduce the risk of depression intensity and relapse by helping you become aware of your thoughts, feelings, and actions. Mindfulness meditation helps you to listen to the thoughts behind feelings that guide your actions. In this way, you become aware of your assumptions about yourself, your world, and your future. In time, negative thoughts become less automatic, and the feelings connected to them also become less painful, self-destructive, and depressing. You may become more aware of the schemas that are keeping you feeling depressed, above and beyond your feelings of grief.

When you practice mindfulness, keep in mind the various automatic thought patterns discussed earlier in this chapter. As you observe your thoughts, try to relate them to these patterns. Are you engaging in any one process more than others? Are your feelings colored by a particular way of thinking or understanding other people? How do your cognitive biases affect your perception of the world, and how does this make you feel? How does your body feel when you think certain thoughts or have particular feelings? Where in your body are you storing your distress and tension? How does your posture adjust with each thought, each feeling, and each observation? How does your breathing change as you think a certain thought, or feel a certain feeling? These observations enable you to learn how your body, your actions, and your emotions are closely related to how and what you think.

By regularly practicing mindfulness in this way, you can learn how to notice what you are thinking, before you feel it. At first, this realization may seem overwhelming or pointless, but keep in mind that these feelings of powerlessness are also an inherent part of depression. In time, though, understanding how your thought processes, emotions, physical sensations, and actions are interconnected becomes liberating. You learn that you play an active role in how you construct your world and respond to it, and you can guide yourself to healthier ways of thinking as you go along in this endless process.

Mindfulness meditation changes depression, and even reduces the chance of its return, by allowing you to observe your mental short-cuts—automatic assumptions and conclusions—not only while you are meditating or performing mindful activities but also in your daily life. You begin to catch problematic thought patterns as they happen. Even-tually, you become able to deconstruct or disassemble a depression-causing schema, and you empower yourself to construct a healthier, more balanced outlook on yourself, your world, and your future.

Making Sense of Depression in Grief

The key point to take from the discussions in this chapter is that, although depression and grief have a lot in common, there are important differences between the two. In order to deal with depres-sion and maintain a healthy, positive perspective, it is crucial to know how the mind works when it is depressed, be aware of the messages you are sending yourself, and be conscious of how these messages and assumptions make you feel. The practice of mindfulness and mindful activities is indispensable for helping you carry out these tasks.

If you are depressed, remember that there is no shame in being one of the nearly 75 million people (nearly 25 percent of the popula-tion) in the United States who suffer from depression. In overcoming depression, just as in journeying through grief, you will learn a lot about yourself, your relationships, and your underlying assumptions about life. Many of the people I have worked with come to view their depression as a turning point in their lives, a moment in which they were forced to learn more about themselves and their world than they had ever thought possible. Ultimately, what matters most is not whether or not you have or have had depression, but the role that depression plays in your life—what it *means* to you and how you respond to it. People have the potential to make intense, life-changing decisions during the course of depression, just as they do with grief.

This transformation is part and parcel of grieving mindfully—overcoming emotional obstacles and hardship in order to live a fuller life.

8

Learning from Grief

The journey through grief, as well as through depression, can seem circular in many ways. You may feel better for moments, only to find yourself feeling depressed all over again. You may feel as if you've been through the worst of the pain, only to reexperience its intensity all over again.

In working through depression both personally and professionally, I have observed that often people hit "rock bottom" before they begin to feel better again. It is at this very crucial point that you begin the journey out of depression. During this time, you will probably find it particularly helpful to have an established relationship with a therapist to help guide you through the process of change.

Many of the people that I have worked with emerge from their travels through grief, and the depression that often accompanies it, radically changed. I am continually reminded of how through grief and depression our identities can change and, when done mindfully, grow in beautiful directions. This is not a glorification of your grief or your suffering. Rather, change, growth, and transformation happen in the process of *recovering* from depression, in *journeying through grief*, in experiencing the ups and downs, and in continuing to be aware of the difficult emotions, even when you feel that the burden may be too great.

TRAINING THE MIND

As part of the cultivation of radical acceptance, Tibetan Buddhism offers a group of teachings that encourage you how to see difficult relationships and hardships in your life as spiritual guides. These teachings, called "Lojong" or "mind training," were developed in India and Indonesia during the tenth and eleventh centuries, prior to their introduction to Tibet by Dipamkara Atisha in 1042 C.E.

The Role of Compassion

Many of the Lojong texts challenge our notions of suffering and hardship, good and bad. The basic premise of the Lojong teachings is that a main purpose of our lives is to learn and practice compassion toward all beings, including ourselves. Compassion in this context is the spirit of unconditional welcoming, of giving love by opening up to your own or someone else's hardship and suffering. In the Buddhist tradition, the spiritual path is built, brick by brick, by acts of compassion and generosity.

You can always find new depths to your compassion. Even though you may think that you are compassionate, like most people, you probably judge yourself and others and favor certain people over others. In the course of your life, you have probably had "enemies" who became your friends, and "friends" who became enemies. You may have secretly wished hardship on these enemies, while wishing good things for those who were your friends—only to have these people switch sides. The reason for all of this back-and-forth? We usually find it easier to be compassionate and kind toward ourselves when we are happy, and toward others when we consider them to be our friends.

Similarly, you may have felt spiritually validated during happy times, and spiritually abandoned during depression and hardship. Why? We despair or feel wronged when faced with difficult times and challenging relationships. Paradoxically, it is precisely these difficulties in your life and relationships that offer you the opportunity to practice and learn great compassion.

One of the Lojong texts, called the *Eight Verses of Training the Mind,* was composed by Geshe Langri Tangpa. These verses, which embody the essence of the Lojong teachings regarding how to practice and cultivate compassion in the midst of hardship and suffering, challenge us to view our suffering, and the actions of others, as the most fertile ground in which to plant the seeds of compassion.

In order to do this, you need to appreciate that most of your spiritual growth occurs not when you are at ease, comfortable in your life and your relationships, but when you are suffering. The Lojong teachings ask you to break from your habituated ways of looking at life and your relationships—your automatic thoughts and schemas— to see where compassion can fit in.

Compassion is easy when you are surrounded by loved ones, and when life is going well. Your heart feels open when it is happy or comfortable. The real challenge to living a spiritual and mindful life is having compassion toward others and ourselves during difficult times, such as when you feel depressed, anxious, irritated, or angry. What is taught by the Lojong teachings is the importance of bringing a compassionate sense of spirituality into all of our difficult times and relationships.

One of the verses mentions that when someone we love causes us to feel badly, we must see them as our spiritual teacher. For instance, can you view a driver who cuts you off in traffic as a spiritual friend? The person who cuts ahead of you in a line? Someone who treats you badly? A friend or family member who lets you down?

In these examples, compassion looks like the most difficult path. Yet it is precisely in these situations that compassion is needed the most. Each of these instances reminds us of how difficult compassion can be, but how much it is needed in our daily lives.

Understanding Compassion

People often confuse compassion with pity. However, compassion is much more than feeling sorry for someone, or commiserating with them. The word *compassion* is made up of two parts: *com*, meaning "with," and *passion*, which connotes emotion, energy, or intense activity. *Compassion* implies an active sharing of an experience. In short, it is the active alleviation of suffering by sharing your presence with someone else.

When you are depressed or experiencing acute grief, your efforts to be compassionate may actually be attempts to distract yourself from your own pain by focusing on the sufferings of others. You may devote yourself to another person's needs in an attempt to leave your own grief by the wayside. You may even begin to radically accept physical or emotional abuse. When this happens, you wind up feeling that you have no dignity or self-respect—you become burned out. Many of the people I have worked with have found themselves becoming consumed by feelings of low self-worth, inadequacy, guilt, anger, and resentment as they try to be more "compassionate." In the midst of depression and acute grief, it is easy to make yourself the last priority, placing the needs of others above your own. Ironically, though, it is particularly important during these times that true compassion feed into a sense of healthy self-esteem, rather than a loss of spiritual or emotional dignity.

Healthy compassion involves exploring your own relationships and your own experience with suffering. In time, this mindfulness of your relationship to suffering can give you an appreciation of your life and relationships, and those of others. Grief reminds you of how precious and fragile life is, and how any relationship can change. The Lojong teachings are asking you to see this fragility as a call to practice healthy compassion, and to plant the seed of compassion in every relationship, good or bad.

The Alchemy of Equanimity

The Lojong teachings ask us to see difficult times as opportunities to practice equanimity and radical acceptance. They are particularly challenging because they ask us to maintain focus on the positive potential of our existence particularly when we feel distress. The teachings ask you to notice when you are becoming self-absorbed in the midst of your sufferings, great and small, and to utilize instead the spiritual and transformative potential of this suffering. Focusing on the spiritual aspects of pain changes your habitual attitude—the one that tells you that you must hate those who cause you harm, and that when you feel hurt, it is wrong. These teachings are reminiscent of the First Noble Truth—we all suffer, and our suffering is natural.

The Lojong teachings ask that you cultivate an attitude that welcomes hardship—mental, emotional, spiritual, and physical suffering—as a spiritual teacher, an opportunity to learn who you are, who you want to be, and what your core values are. The reason for this is that when we suffer we tend to appreciate the power, preciousness, and importance of life, relationships, and our spiritual beliefs. We cherish the power of compassion. When we are doing well, we are more likely to take these things for granted and have a narrower capacity for spiritual learning.

It is important to remember that the Lojong teachings do not ask us to seek out suffering in order to facilitate spiritual growth. Instead, they teach us how to navigate the pain that naturally unfolds—life's unforeseen and inevitable hurdles. If you search out pain and suffering, you are not practicing Lojong, but what I see as spiritual masochism.

Grief as Teacher

Suffering can bring you to a place of profound mindfulness about your relationships and your spiritual beliefs. While your loved one may not have hurt you directly or intentionally, the loss of that loved one and your shared relationship certainly does hurt. In the context of grief, then, the person, and by extension the relationship, can be your spiritual teacher. Being aware of how your loved one lived, what his or her role was in your life, and how you are experiencing the loss of that person can turn your grief journey into a vehicle for your spiritual growth. Without this person's presence in and loss from your life, you would not have this unique opportunity to appreciate life and love, and seek out personal growth.

Using the pain of loss as a spiritual teacher, you begin to cultivate a sense of gratitude toward what you are feeling and experiencing. The intense emotional pain of your grief may still hurt. However, as you experience grief mindfully, allowing yourself to feel the twists and turns of the spiral staircase, the triggers and changes in your relationships, and your own personal development, you may eventually come to realize, mentally, emotionally, spiritually, perhaps even physically, that your capacity to grieve—and your capacity to love—are interconnected.

Grieving mindfully can therefore be an affirmation of life and of love. This is the challenge and apparent paradox of the Lojong practice: to experience grief, hardship, and difficulty not as something shameful, impossible, punishing, or toxic, but as an opportunity to learn priceless life lessons.

This approach to loss and suffering in general is certainly not unique to Buddhism; it is part of various spiritual traditions. For instance, in the Bible, the Letter of James says, "whenever you face trials of any kind, consider it nothing but joy, because you know that the testing of your faith produces endurance; and let endurance have its full effect, so that you may be mature and complete, and lacking in nothing" (2–4).

What James is saying has much in common with the Lojong teachings. He is asking us to confront our trials and hardships and see them in a spiritual context rather than according to our own limited perceptions of what is good and bad. Indeed, he is even asking us to see our sufferings as joys!

This spiritual-minded attitude toward suffering changes how you think about life. You may find as you grieve mindfully, aware of what you are thinking and feeling, that you develop a deep confidence in your ability to live through pain. And your capacity to endure the inherent uncertainties of life only becomes more evolved and mature with time, and with diligent practice of mindfulness and mindful activities.

Attitudes Toward Your Spiritual Teacher

Accepting your suffering and your lost loved one as spiritual teachers is a conscious decision on your part. However, when we think of a spiritual teacher, we have an unconscious tendency to put them on a pedestal. You may even find yourself thinking that your loved one was better than you in some way. But when you create an unrealistic, grandiose image of that person, it can easily take away from his or her human qualities, and the day-to-day lessons that your loved one's absence offers you. Idealizing anyone takes away from the reality of who they are: an ordinary person, just like you, capable of making mistakes but also capable of living with extraordinary wisdom and compassion. Idealizing the person you have lost also takes away from your own presence and potential, and the role of other people in your life.

For instance, one of my patients, Esther, grew up as the youngest in a large family of Polish immigrants in New York City in the 1920s. Life was tough from birth. As a child she was overwhelmed by having to take care of the needs of her older siblings, parents, and grandparents. At the age of seventeen, she met Jacob, a fellow immigrant, and they were married a short time later. Unfortunately, Jacob died suddenly of a heart attack when Esther was only thirty-four. Despite her grief, she became more active in her synagogue, finding new vitality in her religion, but also continuing to idealize this marriage, convinced it had been perfect in every way. As the years went on, she became even more consumed by Jacob's death and how it had brought her closer to God. Her children, now fully grown and married, became estranged from her. All she could talk about was their deceased father.

Many years later, she noticed that a man at her workplace, Seth, was courting her. They were married two years later. Now in her sixties, Esther found herself reconnecting with her family and old friends. After nearly thirty years, they were surprised and relieved to have a conversation with her that did not include a mention of Jacob. Unfortunately, Seth died a short time later of cancer. Before his death, he told her that he had been trying to court her for many years before she finally noticed and consented to go out with him. She had been so focused on idealizing Jacob that she had missed a new chapter of happiness that could have been hers.

It is important to realize that the person you are grieving—the relationship that has been affected the most—is still alive, in your own mind. In many ways, grief itself is a continuation of this relationship. What matters now more than the relationship itself is how you choose to remember it, and how you choose to grieve its loss. Understanding that your loss is part of the human experience—how many millions have suffered as you are suffering?—can enrich your current relationships, rather than leave you, like Esther, isolated or disappointed with what you have.

Another attitude that may develop is a feeling of superiority to others because you are grieving mindfully. Or, in developing a spiritual view of suffering, you may feel hardened, perhaps even overconfident at times in your ability to endure pain. You may feel that because of your acceptance of grief as a teacher, you are part of an elite club, one that other people just cannot understand. You begin to romanticize grief and its hard lessons. You may then start to idealize yourself, even at the expense of remaining mindful and open to what life has to offer.

These stumbling blocks—idealizing your loved one or feeling superior—are actually ways of getting away from the reality of your loss.

Thinking of your loved one as a spiritual teacher is not about idealizing who he or she was, or about developing an inflated sense of self-worth because you are developing spiritually. Neither is it a "cure" for the pain of grief. Rather, it is about grieving mindfully—about choosing how you come to terms with your loss. Looking at grief as a spiritual teacher or personal lesson has more to do with how you live your life after loss than any specific characteristics in your personality or that of the person you have lost. Just as that person is a spiritual teacher, so are all of your loved ones and acquaintances. In turn, you yourself are a potential spiritual teacher to everyone you meet. All that is needed is the willingness to learn the lessons of loss.

Struggles, Resilience, and Gratitude

What psychologists are learning is that in order to become resilient in the face of suffering—in order to endure suffering, and emerge from the journey—one must engage in a struggle, which is part of the process of climbing the spiral staircase. This struggle may not seem like it has a beginning, middle, or an end but is the path of your emotions along the spiral staircase—the milestones, the triggers, the ups and downs.

Without this struggle, without the tears of grief, the long days and endless nights, there is nothing to be passionate about or fight for, only an unfeeling numbness. For better or for worse, in order to grow spiritually from suffering, we must deal with suffering and feel the fire of emotional pain. (Of course, this is not to say that you should keep yourself depressed, or not seek treatment if you feel you need it.)

The Lojong teachings offer us a way to face our struggles with resilience in mind. One of the things that always strikes me about these teachings is the profound gratitude with which they encourage us to live our lives. Adversity, suffering, distress, bitterness, and anger—these are the dark clouds that seem to poison our days. Yet we are challenged to be grateful for these hardships as vehicles for our spiritual growth. Your grief can be one of the most intense spiritual teachers you will ever have. In enduring grief, if you are to grow from the experience and learn to cherish your life, your relationships, and your potential, it is only appropriate to feel thankful toward the experience and the loved one you have lost.

Gratitude is not an alternative to experiencing pain, but a means by which to endure pain. It is all too easy to use spirituality as a cop-out, as a way of denying the reality and magnitude of our suffering. You may even be tempted to feel immune to suffering, using a spiritual identity as a way of numbing yourself to your very human vulnerability to pain. However, in going back to the Lojong teachings, you are reminded: you hurt badly. You don't need to try too hard, or deny the reality of the loss, but experience loss mindfully, in its unpredictable entirety.

Choices in the Face of Suffering

When we talk of being grateful to your lost loved one, and to your grief, we are talking about moving into the heart of grief, rather than stepping away from it. What we are talking about is courage. Being able to endure suffering is courageous in itself. There is no courage without fear, and no fear without distress. This is another of the mysteries of suffering—that we find spiritual meaning, and therefore spiritual endurance, in the face of suffering by moving *into* our emotions rather than away from them. We are all guaranteed to experience suffering. We cannot choose to escape it. However, we can be courageous in our choice to face suffering.

Personal growth or spiritual evolution is one of the most personal choices a person can make. Your spiritual growth, although interconnected with the presence of others and an awareness of the preciousness of all of our relationships, is your own task. Spiritual growth is something that you alone are responsible for. Fundamentally, spiritual growth is always available to us, in everyday encounters, in all of our relationships, in our emotions, even in our thoughts.

The Dalai Lama Teaches at Tabo Monastery

In 1996, I traveled to a remote part of the Indian Himalayas called Spiti Valley to attend a ten-day teaching given by His Holiness the Dalai Lama at the ancient Tabo Monastery. The teaching was being given in this majestic but dusty valley twelve thousand feet above sea level, just a few miles from the Tibetan border. The setting was spectacular. Tall, snow-capped peaks surrounded the valley. The tiny Spiti River flowed like a glass ribbon through the valley, crystal clear and icy from the mountains and snowmelt. A small village straddled the one-thousand-year-old Tabo Monastery.

The journey to Tabo was long. After the eighteen-hour flight to Delhi, I rode an overnight bus to the North Indian town of Manali. From Manali, I spent more than two days in a jeep following steep, treacherous mountain roads. The valleys below were littered with vehicles that had failed to complete the journey. In many cases, their occupants' sun-bleached bones were clearly visible. As we neared Tibet, we saw some nomads coming in from over the border, having traveled by yak for miles to receive the teaching.

At Tabo, the accommodations were basic. Most of us stayed in surplus Indian army tents with a dirt floor. There was no plumbing, the weather alternated between searing heat and icy cold, and choking dust storms often filled the valley.

Sitting under the shade of the monastery canopy during the teaching, the Dalai Lama was clear and concise, as always. One of his comments referred to the arduous journey to Tabo, and the daily hardships most of us were facing there. "It would be a waste," he said, "to journey all this way to this remote part of the world so you can attend this teaching if it had no effect on your life at all. What this journey and this teaching means is completely up to you—coming here is not enough. You must live your life differently from this day forward."

What the Dalai Lama was telling us is that simply being present for the spiritual teaching—any spiritual teaching—is not enough. We must make the choice to use the experience and the wisdom it offers to live a better life.

Choosing Compassion

Accepting the spiritually and personally transformative potential of suffering is one of your many choices in grief. You can go down other roads—denial, isolation, addiction, spiritual stagnation. But by grieving mindfully, with the practice of mindfulness meditation and other mindful activities, you make the decision to deepen your daily experience of life. Many of the world's spiritual traditions teach that the life enriched by mindfulness and transformed by suffering ideally leads to a more compassionate existence. By seeing your grief as a spiritual teacher, you develop a sense of gratitude toward it that can arouse a great compassion toward yourself and your loss. However, the nature of compassion is that it must be shared, ripening only when it is directed toward others, especially those people and relationships that we find difficult.

I have often seen firsthand the transformative, compassion-teaching potential of grieving mindfully. As a clinician, I am always humbled and moved when, in the depths of the most profound and intimate suffering, someone who is grieving discovers his or her own capacity to care for others. For example, Sophie's husband, Hiram, was diagnosed with metastatic pancreatic cancer. He endured surgery, chemotherapy, and radiation, but the disease continued to progress. Although their marriage of many years had sometimes been quite difficult, Sophie stood by him, finding endurance in her art and in meditation. After months of fighting a losing battle against the cancer, Hiram consented to being admitted to a local hospice. Sophie remained very active in his care, and she was next to him when he ultimately died.

After a couple of months, having been deeply moved by the compassion of the hospice nurse who had cared for Hiram, Sophie decided to become active in a hospice agency. When I last heard from her, she was helping other caregivers take care of their loved ones during their last days. From the ashes of her marriage to Hiram rose great compassion in her to help other couples live and love in their final days together.

I have found that when people grieve mindfully they become increasingly compassionate. They open their hearts and care for others. They learn to value the power of relationships, of mutual respect. If grief can be experienced mindfully, as a spiritual teacher, then its most profound lesson is compassion.

Choosing When to Practice Your Spirituality

The relationship between mindfulness, compassion, and grief is by no means new. When the Buddha first introduced mindfulness practices, he also introduced practices meant to familiarize us with the ubiquity of loss and death, and lay the ethical foundations of a compassionate life. In laying the foundations of the teachings on mindfulness, the Buddha even asked his disciples to perform mindfulness meditation in charnel grounds, places in South Asia where bodies are publicly cremated. He wanted his students to fully realize how precarious life is, and how loss permeates everything that we hold dear.

While meditating in the charnel grounds, these early practitioners were reminded of impermanence on many levels. On the one hand, they were mindful of the fleeting nature of their mental chatter and emotional states. On the other hand, they were forced to reconcile this tendency of our minds to wander with the constant confrontation with the reality of physical death and decay. After meditating in this way, they were able to fully understand the importance of practicing spiritual ethics and compassion. In being exposed to the dissolution of the body, they also understood the urgency of putting their spiritual teachings into practice.

For most of us, meditating in a charnel ground is out of the question. Such places don't even exist in our society. However, in grieving mindfully, the lesson offered is similar to what you would learn there: life is fleeting, and all that we hold dear may soon decay. Rich or poor, young or old, healthy or ill, none of us is exempt from that fate. Therefore, we cannot procrastinate attending to our spiritual development but must instead try to live a compassionate, meaningful life while we have the chance—at this very moment. We cannot wait for ideal conditions, or easy relationships. Instead, a meaningful life, steeped in compassion, begins where we are, in this very moment, in all of our relationships.

It happens *now*.

By grieving mindfully and appreciating the life-changing power of the suffering from loss, you begin to have a different outlook on your life and your relationships. When this change begins to happen, grief itself becomes transformed into rebirth; it is you who are reborn. It is your relationships with yourself, your world, and the people in your life that become reborn.

In this sense, grief does not end; it changes and, in the process, changes your life. The sharp twists and turns of the spiral staircase gradually soften to reveal the buried treasure of grief—your choice to live your life differently, aware of how precious and precarious life is for all of us. This transformation of grief carries a potent message: that you can use life's inevitable challenges to grow, to become a better person. You have it in you to face hardship and suffer, and in so doing deepen your experience of life. You may not choose to suffer, but you can choose to transform your suffering into a meaningful life.

9

Channeling Grief to Life

Grieving mindfully allows you to accept the many lessons that loss offers. In relating to your grief in this way, you may find that your attitude toward suffering—emotional, physical, psychological, and spiritual pain—also changes. The very meaning of suffering, loss, and especially love all transform together, since these are the issues at the heart of grief. In opening up to the process of inner transformation that is the positive potential of any grief journey, in actively constructing the meaning of your grief, you have the ability to change almost any aspect of your life.

You may feel very depressed, even hopeless at times, but this emotional intensity of grief is actually a manifestation of how intensely you live life and can love others. When appreciated for what it is, the intensity of grief too becomes a teacher, and an engine for transforming your life.

BRINGING HOME THE LESSONS OF GRIEF

It is extremely important to remember that the lessons of grief are at their most potent not when they are being learned, but when they are being integrated into your life. It is one thing to read about these ideas, but it is quite another thing to put these ideas into practice. Grief has the power to radically change your life, to encourage a more meaningful, richer life, but only when its lessons are manifested in the way you live your life every day. This means becoming a more active and more mindful participant in your life.

One of the hardest steps in this process can be putting the lessons of grief into practice. Many people I have worked with have a passive appreciation of the concept of mindfulness and the positive transformation of suffering long before they integrate these ideas into their everyday life. By exploring specific areas of their lives, they help this passive appreciation to develop into a more active, dynamic process. It becomes an invigorating, life-affirming task, even though there are still many emotional ups and downs along the way.

In order to help you explore and prioritize ways in which your life can change and improve, try to answer the following questions on a piece of paper, or in your journal:

1. What are my emotional triggers—which people, what places, what activities remind me of the intensity of my loss?

2. How has my relationship to these triggers changed?

3. What do I do differently after my loss that helps me feel invigorated, or in touch with my life's purpose? How have I changed?

4. Are there negative habits or routines that I have developed, or old habits I would still like to break?

5. How do I structure my time? What healthy activities am I doing?

6. How has my diet changed? How can I go about taking better care of my body? What kind of exercise can I do?

7. How have I grown spiritually?

8. When my loss was more recent, what kind of person did I want to be? How am I closer to being the person I wished I could be? How am I different? How am I closer to being the person I want to be in general? What do I need to do differently?

9. What am I putting off that would improve my life and help me be the person I want to be? Am I cultivating mindfulness in my life? If not, why am I putting this off?

10. If I had to go through grief all over again, what would I do differently? How would I enact the lessons this loss has taught me?

11. Are there moments in the recent past in which I passed up the opportunity to put the wisdom of my grief and compassion into practice? What obstacles stood in my way? How can I overcome these obstacles in the future?

12. Are there things that I do every day that could be enriched with greater mindfulness or greater compassion?

I suggest that you review these questions at regular intervals, but especially after you go through a period of acute grief. The raw intensity of acute grief, even months after your initial loss, brings with it a vulnerability to change, and a reminder of the preciousness of life, relationships, and love. When you have this awareness, your spiritual potential—your life's purpose—is at its most accessible because your identity, your ego, is left unguarded and is unable to block your inner growth.

THE POTENTIAL OF INSTABILITY

One of the reasons that loss can feel so overwhelming is that it disrupts many components of your identity all at once. The loss of a loved one hurts because a relationship that formed a cornerstone of your experience of the world is no longer there. It's as if someone removed all of the familiar landmarks in your neighborhood. In this loss, your identity becomes unstable; you feel an eerie sense of life going on, yet being radically different. At times, this can make you feel disoriented or confused because you are no longer able to operate with the same assumptions. The practice of mindfulness meditation and mindful activities can help you to retain a sense of equanimity and purposeful cohesion through this tumultuous time.

We usually think of instability in our identity as being a bad thing, something to avoid. But any event or situation that shakes our identity actually offers us an opportunity to reassess and further refine who we are and how we want to live. Moreover, in grief, there is no choice—loss is something that can happen without your permission or approval, and without any warning. One of the facets of the pain of grief is the pain of instability, of not knowing what you can count on anymore because your world has been shaken by impermanence and separation.

The goal of grieving mindfully is to use this instability for a purpose. In your practice of mindfulness meditation and mindful activities during grief, the emotional, mental, and spiritual instability that accompany loss become the fuels for a reawakening into the preciousness of life and love—at the heart of which is a personal, spiritual renaissance. The life that receives the lessons of grief is always one that has been spiritually transformed.

MINDFULNESS AND SPIRITUALITY

What is meant by *spirituality*? The word, like the word *God*, does not fully describe what it refers to. As I see it, spirituality is a personal process, one that is constantly unfolding and evolving. Spirituality is distinct from religion in that spirituality is personal, whereas religion is a shared faith or set of beliefs. Spirituality has more to do with your own personal relationship with whatever helps you feel connected with the positive power of life. For many people, this means a connection with God. However, you don't have to believe in God to be spiritual. Many of the people I have worked with find a sense of spirituality in nature, in relationships, or in performing everyday tasks. For example, one of my patients feels closest to her sense of spirituality while working in her garden. The process of putting on her work gloves and getting her tools ready is a ritual that orients her mind toward her task. For her, spirituality has less to do with belief than with how she is experiencing life.

Many definitions of spirituality rely on a sense of the "sacred," as opposed to the "profane." There really is no such distinction when seen from a mindfulness perspective. When you engage in the practice of mindfulness, you notice the silent weight of *all* of your experiences. Thoughts come and go. Emotions rise and fall. Your breath maintains a continuous thread. You may experience a flash of clarity, a fleeting glimmer of peace, triggered by the most unpredictable thought or feeling. Because all of your life is grist for the mill of mindfulness, everything you experience in mindfulness becomes special, maybe even "sacred." When the session is over, you may slowly forget how powerful it felt to be silent and witness the simple act of swallowing, breathing, or adjusting your posture. You forget how it can feel to simply exist in the clear awareness of the present moment. In practicing mindfulness regularly, you slowly begin to appreciate that there is nothing especially "sacred" because *everything* is especially sacred!

What happens with the regular practice of mindfulness is an equanimity not only toward your own thoughts and feelings, but also toward others, and even toward life itself. Equanimity does not make a distinction between sacred and profane but is open and accepting toward everything equally. Good and bad meditation sessions, the ups and downs of life's continuous journey, your own spiral staircase of grief—with regular mindful awareness, everything becomes a drop in the bucket of your own spiritual fulfillment. Mindfulness helps you to nurture this nondualistic perspective by using every experience as an opportunity to draw your awareness into the immensity of the present moment.

Religion versus Spirituality?

Many of the people that I work with call themselves spiritual but not religious. There is no contradiction in this at all. Religion can be understood as an outward cultural and even institutional entity. Spirituality can often mean the way you experience religion as an individual, or the way you relate personally to certain teachings or beliefs.

The differences between religion and spirituality are often misunderstood, further confusing the sometimes polarized opinions about the two. In my opinion, our society has seen a tremendous backlash against and disillusionment with "Western" religions. It even seems as though it's currently hip to be Buddhist, or otherwise identify with some "exotic" or "esoteric" practices, in order to distance oneself from traditional belief systems. This whole struggle over religion and spirituality is in many ways unnecessary and may even be self-defeating. For many people, denouncing religion is almost a point of pride, as if abandoning or denouncing religion is somehow a badge of honor, or proof of maturity or intelligence. Many people give up entirely on religion without first trying to infuse their religious upbringing with what they have learned spiritually, and their own ways of feeling connected to the world and all life.

My own attitude regarding religion is that it is often extremely helpful to have a group of fellow seekers, or a community with which to share one's spiritual beliefs, and a delineated path toward a goal. Structuring your beliefs, and your meditation practice, in this way helps you to track your progress toward the goal. Otherwise, you might wind up floating aimlessly in the open seas of your own mind and ego.

If you belong to a religious tradition, it is possible, and I believe ideal, for you to fold your spiritual beliefs into this tradition. As His Holiness the Dalai Lama says repeatedly when he teaches to Westerners, you don't have to become a Buddhist to benefit from Buddhism; any spiritual teaching can inform and deepen the practice of your own religion. You don't have to be Buddhist, or belong to any religion, to practice mindfulness. There is nothing wrong with being religious or not being religious. The way we practice our spirituality is unique to each person. From a Buddhist perspective, what matters most is that you have a sense of purpose and meaning in your life that helps you cultivate wisdom and compassion.

A parable in the *Lotus Sutra* illustrates this point. This ancient Buddhist text formed a pivotal role in the development of Mahayana Buddhism, especially in China. One of its chapters talks about the spiritual teachings, life's spiritual lessons, or Dharma, as being like a giant rain cloud that passes over a valley. The cloud drops water on all of the plants and herbs of the valley equally. Each plant drinks its fill, sometimes more than another plant, sometimes less, but always enough. Each plant is unique. The rain quenches all of their thirst, equally—unconditionally.

THE SPIRITUAL PATH OF GRIEF

In channeling the intensity of grief into your spiritual life, it can be easy and tempting to lose perspective of the fact that you are still grieving. This is especially true when you first connect with your grief on a spiritual level; the intensity of your distress may rapidly diminish, resulting in a very natural tendency to try to step away from grief and use spirituality to "feel better." When the inevitable pain of the spiral staircase reasserts itself, you may wind up feeling abandoned by your beliefs, your ability to cope, and your ability to find meaning in your pain. You then become disillusioned, discouraged, and perhaps even more depressed. The initial rush of a revitalized spiritual existence seems to give way to normal, everyday suffering.

Remember that spirituality in grieving is not a "cure" and should not be used as anesthesia. There is no cure for loss—it has already happened, and loss is inevitable in all of our lives. Spirituality and suffering are interdependent. When you are happy, you feel great, and there is no reason for you to ask life's deeper questions or be motivated to engage in a spiritual practice. But when you suffer, you ask these questions and strive with greater intensity to improve your condition. Spirituality is therefore simply an orientation that helps you navigate through your suffering. Despite your spiritual awakening, you are still suffering and there is nothing wrong with you for doing so.

"Why Me?"

I often find that many people unconsciously assume that by leading righteous and spiritual lives they can avoid tragedy and pain. When they inevitably confront emotional or existential pain, as all of us do, they give up believing in a just or fair world, or a compassionate and merciful God. Sometimes, the loss in itself is so tragic and cruel that they may feel that God is not only unfair but also sadistic. How could spirituality possibly make any sense in the face of such suffering?

Perhaps the best-known Western example of this type of scenario is the Book of Job in the Bible. Job, who worshipped God faithfully, had a large, loving, and prosperous family, and Satan believed that Job worshipped God only because of the status and comfort Job had achieved in life. In order to test this theory, Satan caused Job to lose all that mattered to him—his family, his wealth, even his health. In the end, Job did not renounce his spirituality by cursing God, but asked, "why?" The answer Job was given—in fact the answer that we all seem to find at some point or another—is that the answers to all of our "whys" are not as important as *what* we decide to do with our lives and our spiritual potential. The Book of Job seems to imply that the world is not fair at all. Immense tragedy and loss can find us at any moment, sometimes for no good reason. Living a just, spiritual life does not exempt you, or anyone, from suffering. Instead, it prepares you for the inevitability of loss.

When loss is especially tragic and senseless, there seem to be only two roads that people take. They either come away from their loss with renewed investment in their spiritual faith, or they give up their beliefs entirely. In either instance, what is happening is a change of beliefs. Either you can use your spiritual beliefs to accommodate for tragic, senseless loss, or you cannot.

When people lose their sense of spirituality because of loss, they also seem to give up hope. There seem to be no answers for why or how something like this could have happened. However, even if there were answers, they would probably never be sufficient to make the loss comprehensible or offer us comfort. Remember the lesson of Job: even if we could ask the ultimate authority for the reason we suffer, the answer might not be something we could comprehend or find solace in. The only certain answer in the face of loss is not how or why it happened, but what the nature of your life afterward will be.

During part of my clinical training in palliative care, I worked with a remarkable man who, with elegant simplicity, taught me the futility of asking, "Why me?" Carlos, the cornerstone of his family, had a loving wife and two beautiful children. They were all very active in their local church and led full, rich lives. They were a happy family.

One morning, two years before I met him, Carlos woke up and realized that he could not move his legs. He had become paralyzed, suddenly and without explanation. Extensive medical tests confirmed that he had contracted an extremely rare neurological disease, one that puzzled his doctors even after his death. The disease caused the paralysis to spread throughout his body over the course of two and a half years, so eventually Carlos had to depend on a respirator, unable to move his head or even clear his throat. I asked him if his active spiritual beliefs had prepared him for his suffering. He nodded, "Yes." I inquired whether he ever asked, "Why me?" His expression changed to a pensive stare. Then he mouthed, "Why not me?" and smiled.

With those simple words, Carlos taught me that none of us escapes loss. To lose our faith when we are hit by loss is to stop searching for our personal sense of meaning in life.

Understanding Your Spiritual Development

Everyone, spiritual or not, will suffer countless losses and evidence of impermanence during their lives. Just as everyone inhales and exhales, the tides always come in and out, the seasons change, and all of us eventually die. There is no avoiding this fate. Developing a spiritual life does not transform you from human to superhuman, infallible, healthy, favored by God and therefore immune to normal or even exceptional human sufferings. Instead, nurturing your spirituality deepens your experience of being human. You may still be neurotic, "imperfect," and quirky. You may still get angry, irritated, and jealous. You may still get annoyed at traffic, or sleep through your alarm in the morning. Awakening to the spiritual potential of grief is not the end of your journey—it is a new beginning to your life. There is still a lot of work to do. You will still be a unique individual, subject to emotional ups and downs and the random events that color all of our lives.

The intensity of grief, when channeled into a spiritual and mindful life, can be an extremely potent force for change. Many of the people I have worked with have found that they experience a spiritual honeymoon of sorts. When they become attuned to their spirituality, it seems as though grief is over and whatever they apply themselves to—meditation techniques, career, relationships—results in rapid success. Every meditation session seems to lead to profound insight and resolution, every relationship intensifies, and work- and family-related decisions, previously put off for years, suddenly burst forth with exuberance and relief.

It is probably more important at this time than any other to bring yourself back to the real world. This honeymoon period, like all of the facets of our lives, is impermanent. It always ends. Approach the ups and downs of the spiritual journey in the same way in which you have learned to approach grief—mindfully, with equanimity and unconditional acceptance.

Emptiness and Impermanence

As we have learned in previous chapters, one of the corner-stones of Buddhist psychology is the difficulty we all have in accepting the inherently impermanent nature of all phenomena—including thoughts, feelings, identity, relationships, and life itself. The Buddha once described every atom, every fiber of the universe as burning, consumed by the flames of desire and longing for permanence, plea-sure, comfort, and glory in the face of ceaseless change. We all look for the stability in the ground beneath our feet, but we find only shift-ing sand, especially while we grieve. Our yearning for coherence and stability in grief burns uncontrollably.

The realization of the radical impermanence of all phenomena is part of a much larger teaching on *shunyata,* or emptiness. Rather than existing as something "out there," or only in our minds, the universe is empty—empty of our concepts and expectations, empty of objective explanation, empty of our biases and beliefs, empty of our individuality, empty of our assumptions, and empty of our notions of justice and fairness. You may catch a glimpse of the immensity of this emptiness when you practice mindfulness.

Teachings on emptiness state that humans exist not as separate agents of action, but as interconnected and interdependent beings exchanging thoughts, feelings, experiences, and atoms. We are all dependent on everyone else for every aspect of our existence. Think of all of the human labor that goes into everything you experience during the course of your day—who put together your alarm clock, and where did the raw materials and technology come from? Who grew the food you eat? Who made the clothes you wear? Who built the home you live in? Where did these things come from? When you meditate on how much we all rely on each other just to get through our morning routines, emptiness and interdependence are not esoteric concepts. They are the mind-boggling realities that penetrate every aspect of our existence.

Just as the universe is empty, so are our personal identities (see chapter 3). The same is true of our spiritual identities. During your spiritual honeymoon you may feel like saying, "Aha! I've finally arrived!" but in fact there was never anywhere for you to go. As the great Buddhist teacher Nagarjuna said, there is no coming, no going. It has always been right here.

Your spiritual identity is empty of your notions of progress and failure. Like grief, it simply *is*, in all of its intricacy and unpredictability. You may take five steps forward, and ten steps back. You may take ten steps forward and three steps back. If you create too many expectations about your spiritual identity, you lose perspective on the spiral staircase nature of spiritual progress, which is fraught with many, many ups and downs.

I find that when people become invested in these initial spiritual honeymoon experiences, they often abandon their spiritual path when the honeymoon ends. Spiritual texts, meditation experiences and techniques, insights and realizations all become like souvenirs of a trip to an exotic land. Rather than a practice that continues to enrich and deepen your daily life, spirituality becomes a quaint idea that no longer provides a quick emotional fix, or immediate return on your investment. The spiritual life becomes a discrete, stand-alone, commodified activity instead of a here-and-now practical lifestyle.

It is especially important to remain mindful of emptiness and equanimity during these initial, tentative, sometimes outrageously successful first steps of the spiritual journey in grief. It is all too easy to develop an emotional tolerance to spiritual insights and experiences and then give up when these insights and experiences no longer seem to be as rich. The spiritual life is a long-term task, not one gained from quick fixes and soothing words. It too has ups and downs, often for no apparent reason.

The Importance of Practice

Because of the unpredictability of spirituality itself in your life, almost all of the texts that speak of mindfulness emphasize the importance of having a regular practice.

All too often, many of the practices presented in this book—meditation, spirituality, mindfulness—are seen as balms, practices that can help soothe your pain, or the very nature of which can help ease your suffering. But in truth there is nothing particularly soothing about these ideas—unless they are practiced regularly. You must practice to gain any benefit. I cannot emphasize this enough. Although you may read many books, what really matters is making these practices concrete, down-to-earth, and, most important, your own. Simply having this book, or a hundred books, on your bookshelf will not be enough.

If you have not yet established a daily routine that incorporates some element of spiritual and psychological self-care, such as meditation or mindful activities, journaling, artwork, or gardening, now is the time to do so. If you have not experienced a spiritual honeymoon but are having a hard time with the practice, this too is reason to establish a firm routine of mindfulness sessions.

In establishing and *maintaining* a daily self-care routine, you build an epitaph of self-improvement over the loss of your relationship. Your spiritual journey through grief becomes a memorial to your loss, to your relationship. It is a way of honoring your loss. Even though loss is inevitable, using the occasion for improving and enriching your life is something that only you are empowered to do. No one can do this for you. Unlike loss, spiritual growth is not guaranteed to any of us but instead requires a lot of hard work, patience, and perseverance. Loss can provide you the motivation for establishing this goal, but you alone are responsible for maintaining progress along this path.

By harnessing the spiritual potential of grief, you may find that you become more tolerant of the twists and turns of the spiral staircase. Continue to approach spirituality in much the same way you have learned to approach grief—mindfully. In channeling your grief into a spiritual life, you will find that other parts of your life begin to change. Your life becomes more meaningful.

BRINGING THE LESSONS OF GRIEF TO RELATIONSHIPS

One of the most common and yet profound ways that grief changes lives is in the realm of relationships, the very place where grief begins. I have not met a single person who has gone through grief without finding that their other relationships have also been transformed. These changes can sometimes be difficult to predict. People you may have considered close may become distant. Those who were distant may become close. As you think about this idea, ask yourself: who has stepped forward to be closer to you, and who has surprisingly, perhaps painfully, stepped back?

I find that life changes in grief translate into sometimes profound changes in your relationships. You may find that the friends and family members whom you consider to be the closest to you change. Those who can accept your life as a spiritual journey, probably the same people who were able to accept your suffering, become closer to you. They are supportive of your growth, your pain, and your search for meaning in suffering. As these relationships change, they often deepen. Because they are built on the foundation of loss and suffering, these relationships start from a place of deep, emotional sharing, maybe even unconditional love. They are based on the mindful awareness of our human vulnerabilities.

If you are feeling isolated, an experience that is frequently part of depression, it may help you to seek out other people who are striving to live a mindful and spiritual existence. It may require extra effort and energy for you to challenge some of the automatic thought patterns that leave you feeling unworthy or unable to be around people, even if you are more spiritually attuned. You may be helped by finding a community of people who share your beliefs, such as a church, synagogue, temple, or mosque. It may mean going to book readings by your favorite authors, or attending lectures or other local events that attract like-minded people. More recently, spiritual communities on the Internet have provided many people I know with the sense of fellowship that is so important on any spiritual path. Spiritual ideas tend to intensify and solidify when they are shared with supportive friends and family members. Do seek out these people, if you haven't already.

As I have emphasized throughout this book, the power of grief can fuel some of the most intense, positive changes in your life. I have seen numerous instances of grief leading to life-changing decisions. Even though the starting point of grief is loss, grieving mindfully—channeling mindfulness and acceptance of loss into resilience—is really about rebirth, and reinvesting in your life.

10

Grieving Mindfully, Living Mindfully

When the emotions of grief first arrive, they are usually unwelcome guests. These emotions seem like an invasion of your personal space, and you cannot wait for these uninvited visitors to leave. But they do not leave. Grief weaves its way into your life, into your relationships, and into your way of seeing the world. As your grief journey progresses, you develop a sense of the rhythm between the alternating intensities of acute and subtle grief and of the twists and turns of the spiral staircase. As time goes on, as you practice mindfulness, as your journey on the spiral staircase continues to unfold, as you grow, grief changes your life and its lessons become part of your identity.

Mindfulness helps you develop a sense of patience with and acceptance of the ups and downs of grief. As you continue on your grief journey, your practice of mindfulness meditation and mindful activities also deepens. This is in part because grief heightens your awareness of life in general, as does mindfulness. Each moment develops a delicate, precious potential that is far beyond our tendency to take "small" things for granted and live in anticipation of future tasks and events.

WHERE GRIEF GOES

In integrating your practice of mindfulness with your grief, you may go through an initial period of success—feeling the magnitude of each relationship, each day, each interaction, and each breath. Or, you may not feel the effects of grieving mindfully for many months. The time frame does not matter. There is no "normal" amount of time required for mindfulness, either in the length of each session or in the number of years you practice. Similarly, despite what some people may tell you, there is no normal amount of time for grief. What is important with both grief and mindfulness is knowing that these are both long-term processes for which there are no shortcuts.

Your pain may gradually lessen, even seeming to be resolved. In opening yourself up to the changes and vulnerabilities that are grief's positive potentials, you will find that the way you see your own life, and the lives of others, has changed. These changes reflect themselves in your lifestyle, your activities, your priorities, your diet, and your relationships, although they may or may not be easy for everyone around you to see.

Learning from Nature

The most burning questions about grief, and about how grief changes your life, have to do specifically with the emotional intensity of grief. What happens to the intense distress that accompanies grief, puts you at risk for depression, and has such life-changing potential?

In physics, the first law of thermodynamics states that energy can neither be created nor be destroyed. Energy can only be transformed. When massive stars many times more powerful than our sun are sucked into and crushed by cosmic black holes, their matter is released back into the universe in plumes of light and energy. The debris of these stars goes on to seed space, creating new stars, new planets, and perhaps even new life. From one of the most destructive forces in the universe come the building blocks and raw materials of life itself.

So too with grief. The energy of grief encompasses all that is your identity. Grief happens physically, emotionally, mentally, spiritually, and interpersonally. It can be seen as a black hole that emerges, often unexpectedly, in your life, but which causes the sowing of the seeds of the rest of your life. In another metaphor, the process of accepting and transforming loss and grief becomes like a forest regenerating itself after a devastating forest fire, which seems catastrophic but is actually part of the natural order of ecosystems. Some trees even produce seeds that can only be opened by the intense heat of fire. By grieving mindfully, you make a commitment to yourself to engage the transformative power of grief with intention. You commit yourself to taking deliberate steps toward your future, ideal self.

Rebuilding Your Life

How you change with grief is an ongoing process. These changes build upon each other. As time goes on, grief makes a seamless transition into your life and your identity. The despair and intense distress of grief gradually ebb and flow, sometimes very slowly fading away into memory. What remains are the life choices you make fueled by the mindful awareness of your thoughts and feelings. Your relationship to yourself, and to those around you, changes. You may be surprised at where you wind up.

For example, many years ago, when I was still a student, I was visiting my parents at their home in South Florida. While I was there, Hurricane Andrew devastated their neighborhood. Every house was seriously damaged, and most of them had to be completely destroyed and rebuilt. The lush Florida landscape was completely gone; not a single leaf was left on a tree.

However, some remarkable things happened after the hurricane. The people in the neighborhood became closer than they had ever been before. Neighbors who hardly knew each other began freely sharing food, water, or a shoulder to cry on. In time, the neighborhood was rebuilt. Each house was built stronger. In fact, many homeowners learned the lesson from the hurricane and rebuilt their homes with a new respect for the power of nature.

For me, the hurricane and the loss of our home was a turning point. Many of our family mementos were destroyed. Many of my own prized possessions were reduced to rubbish. I grieved not only the loss of these material possessions, but also the loss of the sense of safety, in buildings and in nature. After returning to school, I began in earnest to try to integrate this grief into my life.

This very book is an indication that the lessons of the hurricane are still with me. They no longer take the form of pain or suffering; my distress related to Hurricane Andrew has long since faded away. But its lessons remain with me in how I live my life, the work I do, the spiritual beliefs I have. If I had been given the choice to end my feelings of grief immediately after the storm, I would probably have agreed to do so. No one wants to feel pain. However, from a different perspective, I realize that I was provided an opportunity to grieve, and grief provided me an opportunity to grow. If I had been told that the pain felt would eventually lead to the changes in my life that I have experienced, I would probably not have believed it possible.

As time goes on, you too may find yourself awed by the changes in your life. You may even be able to appreciate your experience of loss, to see the silver lining instead of the clouds. You may find that your assumptions about the role of pleasure and pain, distress, depression, and suffering in your life have been changed by grief.

You may find that your understanding of the world has been turned upside down and takes a lot of time to resettle. Or, you may find that the world is as you saw it all along—impermanent and precious. You may experience mindful grieving as a reaffirmation of truths you discovered years ago but perhaps forgot. You may find that grieving mindfully intensifies a perspective on life that you held before but had put aside.

Building a Mindful Life

The process of understanding your assumptions about suffering and loss, and learning the lessons of your grief, may take months or even years. What is important is to approach the concept, the process of grieving mindfully, as you approach your own mind—with patience, acceptance, and unconditional positive regard.

In the *Mahârâhulovâda Sutta*, one of the disciples of the Buddha, named Sariputra, encourages us to develop meditation that is like the earth, water, fire, air, and space. Sariputra talks about how we use each of these elements for both clean and unclean things. For example, we may use water to quench our thirst, or to wash away the filth from our clothes. Whether we consume it or pollute it with dirt, water is indifferent. Water accepts all that we do with it unconditionally. One day you may have an effortless time with your mindfulness practice or the distress of your grief. The next day, you may feel extremely stressed, distracted, and distressed. Throughout these ups and downs, cultivate a practice of mindfulness that accepts you for where you are, however you may feel. Your practice should be like water, which can both satisfy your thirst or wash away dirt. It is with this attitude that you integrate grief into your mindfulness practice, and both of these things into your life.

WHAT HAPPENS TO GRIEF

There are subtle but profound differences between thinking of your grief journey as something you need to tough out and defend against, and thinking of it as something you can grow from. I find that with grief, as is the case with most emotional challenges, it is more helpful and realistic to focus on resilience and hardiness—being able to feel and adapt—rather than on recovery or "getting over it." It is more realistic to conceptualize grief as gradually being folded into your life. That is, grief is not a discrete thing "out there" that you can go through and emerge from, dust off your clothes, and then be on your way.

Grief is a daily challenge to your assumptions about the world. It demands that you accept that loss is a part of all of our lives. Going through grief demands that you abandon the notion that you must always feel good, and that if you don't, you are at fault, incomplete, weak, or unworthy in some way. You are forced to accept loss not just intellectually, but with every aspect of your person, your identity. You must abandon years of looking at distress as weakness, failure, pointless, or absurd. Often in grief, the presence of emotional pain means that there is more right with you than wrong with you!

Grief Transforms How You Live

Grieving mindfully is to accept the hard fact that we don't always grow from feeling good, but most often from those inevitable parts of life that cause us distress. We do not need to seek distress for growth, or hold on to it once it appears. Life seems to provide as much as we need, and sometimes even more than we feel we can handle. Grieving mindfully means embracing ourselves—our thoughts, our feelings, our actions, our spirituality—with a sense of equanimity. With your own practice of mindfulness as the ultimate inner teacher, everything you experience in life—good, bad, painful, delightful—becomes a spiritual teacher, if you allow it to. Everything you experience in life becomes an object of meditation, reflection, and growth. You become closer to being like the water Sariputra describes—capable of unconditional equanimity.

This does not mean rationalizing self-destructive or negative behaviors, or rationalizing your addictions. What unconditional acceptance or equanimity means is allowing yourself the space to experience that which we may find uncomfortable in our limited, individualistic perspective on life. It may mean finally giving up the thing that, deep down inside, you know is unhealthy, by allowing yourself to change. Unconditional acceptance may mean letting in those thoughts that invade your comfort zone because they require positive, life-affirming changes that would mean giving up old habits or addictions, old notions of what is pleasing and what is distressing.

Accepting the Opportunity for Compassion

Most of all, unconditional acceptance means love, for yourself, and for those around you. It means approaching each relationship with the awareness that you may never see this person again. Imagine a world where we all keep this truth in mind. Grief allows for this profound compassion—which we often think of as more than we as individuals can handle. We idealize the great heroes of compassion—Mahatma Gandhi, Mother Teresa, Martin Luther King Jr.—precisely because their deeds seem so out of reach.

But is profound compassion not something we are all capable of? If you grieve, you suffer the pain of loss. If you suffer pain from loss, it is hard proof that you are capable of love, and therefore compassion, forgiveness, and actions of profound yet simple generosity that may begin and end with ordinary interactions: allowing someone ahead of you in line, putting aside a grudge you have been holding on to, smiling at someone you don't know, saying "thank you," taking time to volunteer to help those less fortunate than you, not sweating the small stuff.

The funny thing is that as you help others, you tend to feel better about yourself, the world, and life in general. Giving love is sometimes the most powerful way of receiving healing. In helping others, you grow.

Mindfulness teaches you that it all starts with accepting the precariousness of this very moment. The way that grief can fold itself into your life meaningfully is by awakening compassion based on the realization of impermanence. This is the same fruit of mindfulness—to infuse your daily experience of life with compassion for all beings, beginning with and including yourself.

Mindfulness helps you to feel the preciousness of life by heightening your experience of each passing moment. It is these fleeting moments that form the building blocks of your experience of life. Breathing in, aware. Pausing. Breathing out, aware.

Scattered thoughts in between. Sounds from outside of the room.

Each moment passes with enormity, with pregnant potential.

Sometimes with commentary. Sometimes with unconditional acceptance. Sometimes, fleetingly, with flashes of clarity.

With dignity. With reverence.

In this context, is the presence of grief in your life so unwelcome?

When you learn that this is how grief works, that it only changes but does not end, you may initially feel helpless, or even overwhelmed. However, remember that it is not distress that gets folded into your life. It is your choice to live life differently, to cultivate mindfulness, spirituality, and connectedness to others. What need not end is the willingness to live, to endure, to search for meaning, and to share living.

After Hiram's death, Sophie surprised us all by telling us she was going to work for her local hospice. I had seen her shortly after the death of her husband, and she told me that she was crying almost constantly. Her distress was palpable. But instead of wishing her grief would end, she accepted its presence and used the momentum of her grief to alleviate the suffering of others. Sophie planted within the storm of her acute grief the seeds of a renewed, meaningful life based on compassion for herself and others.

WHERE MINDFULNESS GOES

Mindfulness, like grief, draws your awareness to each moment as it passes by. Mindful awareness, if cultivated regularly, spreads beyond the practice of meditation and related activities. Mindfulness and grief merge into one another, both of them complementing each other in their common cause: to draw you into the potential of your life, moment by moment, thought by thought, feeling by feeling, action by action, breath by breath.

What you will find, if you have not already, is that your search for meaning in loss is actually the same as your search for meaning in life. When you begin this search and become an active participant in the search for your life's meaning, grief becomes a paradox. Although wrapped in pain and sometimes even trauma, loss becomes procreative. Like the legendary phoenix, your life reemerges renewed from the blazing fires of loss and impermanence.

With both grief and mindfulness, there are no finish lines, no trophies, no welcome-home parades. There is the silent witnessing of your own thoughts, your feelings during the alchemy of everyday uncertainty, and the choices you make in life. Your understanding of life—of why we are here, of why we suffer, of the role of suffering in all of our lives—changes.

Hidden Treasure

There is a metaphor that is often used in Buddhist writings, that spiritual teachings are "jewels in rubbish heaps." That is, we often find spiritual lessons and inner growth in parts of our lives where we would least expect them. These spiritual jewels may lie undisturbed underneath layers of pain and sorrow. On any given day, they lurk under the surface of our assumptions about the world. It is only when you suffer loss that you pause to contemplate the roots of suffering, to engage in grief mindfully. You look underneath the layers of sadness, even depression, and find the jewel of a mindful and meaningful existence. These jewels are the changes you make in your life with the heightened awareness—mindfulness—of being alive.

Although these spiritual treasures are different for each person, there is always one common jewel to be found in the rubbish heap of suffering: that we must remember impermanence, and not take a single relationship, a single day of life, for granted.

A Sense of Gratitude

I have worked with hundreds of people and families who have suffered many different types of loss—sudden death, violent death, death from illness, unemployment, divorce, natural disaster, and so on. I often hear people I work with tell me that the changes in their lives brought on by grief are gifts from their lost loved ones, or even from the causes of their loss. As you continue to find jewels along your grief journey, the experience of grief changes from one of despair to one of gratitude, the result of a sense of having used the suffering of loss to better yourself, your life, and the people around you. Your loved one may not even have been able to understand that the meaning of your relationship has achieved loftier goals than either of you could have imagined when you were together. But the ultimate memorial to any relationship you have lost is self-improvement, letting yourself grow, adapt, and change into a better person, integrating the loss into a better life.

The Ultimate Goal

In the original teachings in which mindfulness was presented, practice is stated as "the direct path for the purification of beings, for the surmounting of sorrow and lamentation, for the disappearance of pain and grief, for the attainment of the true way, for the realization of Nirvana" (Nanamoli and Bodhi 1995). Noble goals, indeed. The Buddha himself was declaring that mindfulness is more than a tool, much more than a technology of developing awareness and equanimity. Mindfulness is the foundation of our journey to nirvana, to enlightenment itself.

What is nirvana? In Buddhism, nirvana is considered to be ultimate freedom. Freedom from suffering, freedom from craving, freedom from the endless cycles of birth, old age, sickness, and death. Freedom from the dualisms of self and other, pain and pleasure, attraction and aversion. Freedom from wrong views about ourselves and each other, bad habits, hatred, aggression, and greed.

Nirvana is defined in many different ways, probably because it is hard to describe. The Buddha himself was speechless for weeks after he had experienced nirvana. I understand nirvana to be a state of effortless transcendence, in which there is no longer any distinction between ourselves and others around us. Unconditional compassion and love arise without effort. We are able to see into the ultimate nature of life and death. We are free of our individual limitations.

In descriptions of the Buddha's enlightenment, it is often said that he was able to see all the inhabitants of all worlds everywhere that have ever existed, exist now, and will exist in the future. Individual boundaries dissolved. There was no sense of separation between beings and time. All was unified in the eternal moment that characterizes nirvana.

The Buddha taught that nirvana is within the reach of all of us, as long as we practice mindfulness and compassion. Later, different schools of Buddhism developed differing ideas about the causes of nirvana. Some say nirvana has to be approached step by step. Others say it can happen instantly, unpredictably. But all schools agree that the proper practice of mindfulness and compassion form the center of all paths to nirvana.

When seen in the context of Buddhism and mindfulness, your loss, your grief, can provide you with the ultimate wake-up call: to investigate and realize the nature of life itself. This goal, though it may seem lofty, is within reach. Indeed, the Buddha's own historical journey to nirvana began with a profound disillusionment with life's pleasures, and the emotional shock of having to accept the fragile nature of all aspects of our existence. If you are reading this book, you are probably thinking and feeling many of the same things that the Buddha himself experienced before he began his own spiritual journey.

Why not approach that lofty goal? Why not seek the freedom to live a spiritually enriched and compassionate life? Imagine a world where grief universally meant a call to compassion, gratitude, and awakening, rather than vengeance, anger, or hatred. Injustice, violence, and aggression would surely be much less of a problem. Compassion and gratitude are certainly not purely "Buddhist" goals but instead are the ultimate aim of all of the world's great spiritual traditions—to transform our lives from ones perpetuating ignorance and suffering to lives of meaning and compassion.

In going through your grief journey mindfully, you have all the elements of your own spiritual awakening. You are learning every day—often painfully—about the fluid nature of your identity and your relationships. You can use these realizations to become the person you want to be.

You are learning that grief, like your spiritual journey and most aspects of all of our lives, is fraught with ups and downs, ebbs and flows. One day is happiness, the next sadness. So too with your spiritual journey. On some days it seems like nirvana is just a short distance away. On other days, you feel like an incompetent beginner. What matters is not so much the concept as much as the process.

You are learning how precarious life is. One day, it seems as though you are surrounded by loving family and friends. The next day, you feel totally alone in the universe. You can use this sense of fragility as motivation to carry out wholesome changes in your life, to not waste time, to not put off your own growth and potential as a human being.

You are learning about your assumptions about the meaning of your life. Again, what matters is not so much the concept as much as the process; it is not necessarily finding *the* meaning of life as much as your own search for meaning. And this too can change from one day to the next, from one moment to the next. Some days, the meaning of your life may not be to solve world hunger, or alleviate poverty—it may be simply to appreciate the sunset, or feel the breeze on your face.

The search for meaning in your life is constructed moment by moment, day by day. This is also the lesson of mindfulness. To develop equanimity, unconditional love, and compassion through accepting the presence of emotional, mental, and physical distraction. To use what you have in front of you to overcome suffering, by moving into the heart of the person who suffers. To see the root of your pain in grief as love. To use this love to improve your life, your relationships, and the world around you. To live a rich, compassionate life.

To grasp the revolutionary, spiritual potential of life's inevitable ups and downs.

To seize the vastness of this very moment.

References

American Psychiatric Association. 1994. *Diagnostic and Statistical Manual of Mental Disorders.* 4th ed. Washington, DC: American Psychiatric Association.

Bayrak, T. 2000. *The Name and the Named: The Divine Attributes of God.* Louisville, KY: Fons Vitae.

Benson, H., and I. L. Goodale. 1981. The relaxation response: your inborn capacity to counteract the harmful effects of stress. *Journal of the Florida Medical Association* 68(4):265–7.

Bonanno, G. 2004. Loss, trauma, and human resilience: Have we underestimated the human capacity to thrive after aversive events? *American Psychologist* 59:20–28.

Byock, I. 1997. *Dying Well: Peace and Possibilities at the End of Life.* New York: Riverhead Books.

———. 2004. *The Four Things That Matter Most: A Book about Living.* New York: Free Press.

Davidson, R. , J. Kabat-Zinn, J. Schumacher, M. Rosenkranz, D. Muller, S. Santorelli, F. Urbanowski, A. Harrington, K. Bonus, and J. Sheridan. 2003. Alterations in brain and immune function produced by mindfulness meditation. *Psychosomatic Medicine* 65: 564–570.

Frankl, V. E. 1997. *Man's Search for Meaning.* New York: Pocket Books.

Gyeltsen, G. T. 1989. *Keys to Great Enlightenment.* Los Angeles: Thupten Dhargye Ling Publications.

Harding, S., and K. Thrangu. 2002. *Creation and Completion: Essential Points of Tantric Meditation.* Somerville, MA: Wisdom Publications.

His Holiness the Dalai Lama. 1999. *Lojong: Training the Mind.* Somerville, MA: Wisdom Publications.

Kabat-Zinn, J., L. Lipworth, R. Burney, and W. Sellers. 1987. Four-year follow-up of a meditation-based program for the self-regulation of chronic pain: treatment outcome and compliance. *Clinical Journal of Pain* 2:159–73.

Kato, B., Y. Tamura, and K. Miyasaka. 1990. *The Threefold Lotus Sutra.* Tokyo: Kosei Publishing Company.

Kumar, S., G. Feldman, and A. Hayes. (under review) Change in mindfulness and emotion regulation strategies in an integrative therapy for depression. *Cognitive Therapy and Research.*

Mahoney, M. J. 1991. *Human Change Processes: The Scientific Foundations of Psychotherapy.* New York: Basic Books.

Marlatt, G. A. 2002. Buddhist philosophy and the treatment of addictive behavior. *Cognitive and Behavioral Practice* 9:44–50.

Nanamoli, B., and B. Bodhi. 1995. *The Middle Length Discourses of the Buddha: A Translation of the Majjhima Nikaya.* Boston, MA: Wisdom Publications.

Niemeyer, R. A. 1997. Meaning reconstruction and the experience of chronic loss. In *Living with Grief When Illness is Prolonged,* edited by Kenneth Doka. Bristol, PA: Hospice Foundation of America.

Rando, T. A. 1997. Living and learning the reality of a loved one's dying: Traumatic stress and cognitive processing in anticipatory grief. In *Living with Grief When Illness is Prolonged*, edited by Kenneth Doka. Bristol, PA: Hospice Foundation of America.

Robins, C. J. 2002. Zen principles and mindfulness practice in dialectical behavior therapy. *Cognitive and Behavioral Practice* 9:50–57.

Rogers, C. 1995. *On Becoming a Person*. Boston, MA: Houghton Mifflin Company.

Segal, Z. V., J. M. G. Williams, and J. D. Teasdale. 2002. *Mindfulness-Based Cognitive Therapy for Depression*. New York: Guilford Press.

Shantideva, translated by the Padmakara Translation Group. 1997. *The Way of the Bodhisattva*. Boston, MA: Shambala Publications.

Shulz, R. and L.M. Martire. 2004. Family caregiving of persons with dementia: prevalence, health effects, and support strategies. American Journal of Geriatric Psychiatry 12(3):240–9.

Summers, R. F., and J. P. Barber. 2003. Therapeutic alliance as a measurable psychotherapy skill. *Academic Psychiatry* 27:160–165.

Teasdale, J. D., Z. V. Segal, J. M. Williams, V. A. Ridgeway, J. M. Soulsby, and M. A. Lau. 2000. Prevention of relapse/recurrence in major depression by mindfulness-based cognitive therapy. *Journal of Consulting and Clinical Psychology* 68(4):615–23.

Thrangu, K. 1993. *The Practice of Tranquility and Insight: A Guide to Tibetan Buddhist Meditation*. Boston, MA: Shambala Publications.

Wiser, S., and C. Telch. 1999. Dialectical behavioral therapy for binge-eating disorder. *Journal of Clinical Psychology* 55:755–768.

Zisook, S., S. R. Shuchter, P. A. Sledge, M. Paulus, and L. L. Judd. 1994. The spectrum of depressive phenomena after spousal bereavement. *Journal of Clinical Psychiatry* 55Suppl:29–36.

Sameet M. Kumar, Ph.D., is a psychologist and Buddhist whose areas of expertise include palliative care, spirituality in psychotherapy, mindfulness meditation, stress management and relaxation, and grief and bereavement. He received his doctorate at the University of Miami and has trained with several leading Tibetan Buddhist teachers. He has traveled extensively in India, China, and Tibet and works at the Mt. Sinai Comprehensive Cancer Center in Miami Beach and Aventura, FL, and at the Wellness Community in Miami, FL.

Foreword writer **Jeffrey Brantley, MD,** is a consulting associate in the Duke University Department of Psychiatry in Durham, NC. He is founder and director of the Mindfulness-Based Stress Reduction Program at Duke University's Center for Integrative Medicine, as a spokesperson for which he has given many radio, television, and print media interviews. He is the author of *Calming Your Anxious Mind*.

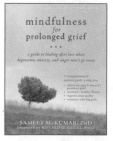